The Nonstop Color Garden

First published in 2014 by Cool Springs Press, an imprint of Quarto Publishing Group USA Inc., 400 First Avenue North, Suite 400, Minneapolis, MN 55401 USA

Cool Springs Press titles are also available at discounts in bulk quantity for industrial or sales-promotional use. For details write to Special Sales Manager at Quarto Publishing Group USA Inc., 400 First Avenue North, Suite 400, Minneapolis, MN 55401 USA.

To find out more about our books, visit us online at www.coolspringspress.com.

ISBN-13: 978-1-59186-605-3

Library of Congress Cataloging-in-Publication Data

Neal, Nellie.
The nonstop color garden : design flowering landscapes and gardens for year-round enjoyment / Nellie Neal.
    pages cm
Includes index.
ISBN 978-1-59186-605-3 (sc)
1. Flower gardening. 2. Gardens--Design. I. Title.
SB404.9.N43 2015
635.9--dc23
                                        2014020695

Acquisitions Editor: Billie Brownell
Project Manager: Madeleine Vasaly
Design Manager: Brad Springer
Cover Designer: Mary Rohl
Layout Designer: Diana Boger
Illustrator: Chandler O'Leary

On the front cover: © iStockPhoto.com/BasieB
On the back cover (from left): Krawczyk-A-Foto/
    Shutterstock; Jean-Pol Grandmont/CC-BY-SA-3.0;
    Guzel Studio/Shutterstock
On the title page (from top): Richard Shiell,
    courtesy Monrovia; freya-photographer/
    Shutterstock; Inomoto/Shutterstock; George Weigel;
    Andre Viette; Liz Ball

Printed in China

10 9 8 7 6 5 4 3 2 1

THE NONSTOP COLOR GARDEN

Design flowering
landscapes and gardens
for year-round enjoyment

Nellie Neal

COOL
SPRINGS
PRESS
Home and Garden Experts™

MINNEAPOLIS, MINNESOTA

Dedication

To my oldest friend, the dear Kathy Greer, and my brilliant daughter, LauraClaire, for making me want to be a better person. As always, to Dave.

Acknowledgments

EVERY AUTHOR WORTH HER SALT knows that each book can only be as good as those who taught her. The lessons of color and its emotional power came to me first from my grandmother, the seamstress and tailor, and my mother, the runway model. Mrs. Oliver taught me to see in line and form and to paint with understanding. She showed me the world of classic design through her voluminous postcard collection. I was transformed by studying under Dr. Robert Reich, for whom the landscape architecture school at Louisiana State University is named. He introduced me to the work of Garrett Eckbo and to the reality of personal expression through garden design. These gurus and the hundreds of people who have invited me into their gardens have given me an invaluable education and inspiration. It has been my privilege to meet and work with amazing landscape architects, professionals who were kind enough to share notes with me and invite me to consult on plants. They are expected to be magicians, to effortlessly birth the client's wildest dreams, and more often than not, they succeed. My sincerest thanks to my editors, Billie Brownell and Madeleine Vasaly, and to their team at Quarto Publishing Group USA.

Contents

Welcome to your nonstop color garden

WHEN YOU WALK INTO a beautiful garden, what do you notice first? The temperature drop in a shady grove on a summer day, a fountain's gurgle, berried hedges on a snowy day, the abundance of spring flowers? Yes, but time and again the *colors* in the garden are what you remember long after because they set the mood for everything else. The power of plants to focus attention and set moods with their colors cannot be understated, but not to be left out, structures and hardscape gain attention here, too. Whether they are meant to fade into the scene or create a focal point, color defines their roles: a wooden shed is a utilitarian joy but a can of paint transforms it into a year-round garden destination. Your feet are down the path to it in a heartbeat, drawn to its color. When you smile to see the first flowering quince (*Chaenomeles*) of spring or thrill as maples (*Acer*) turn in autumn, each time you feel like celebrating lilacs (*Syringa*) or beautyberry (*Callicarpa*), it's their colors that touch your heart. This book will put them close at hand.

All the colors in the organic crayon box are featured here with suggestions for plants in every category to enrich the colors throughout your garden every month of the year. Here's a look at what else you'll find in *The Nonstop Color Garden.*

A neat green carpet lawn and a classic brick hardscape set the stage for this charming border. It displays brilliant use of color to create form within closely related shades using plants that include upright delphiniums in mauve, lilac, and deep blue-purple; rosy flowering onion orbs; pale pink climbing roses; and purple salvia.

7

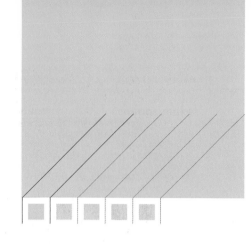

Design inspiration gallery

MUCH OF GARDEN DESIGN is first a broad vision, a concept for coloring space across the seasons. To be successful, the plan exploits that big idea until every detail carries the desired theme. In the best of them, a rewarding design starts as a sparkle in one's eye and becomes tangible for all to enjoy. Landscape architects and garden designers see a year full of color, texture, line, and much more. They translate their visions into plants and hardscape in myriad different ways as you will see in the design inspiration gallery. Gardeners like to be inspired and sometimes can be downright copycats, with good reason. It's perfectly acceptable to take good ideas home, even take photos, and then make them your own.

When you explore a pleasing design, the math and geometry may be complex or minimalist, yet it's always coherent in its own way. The plants and colors fit together; their placement and hue has an inherent sense of rightness. You can find fabulous color everywhere, but the moods and styles of botanic gardens and residential landscapes offer wildly diverse possibilities for your interpretation.

This chapter offers excellent examples of public and private gardens in the lower forty-eight US states, from coast to coast and north to south in all seasons. The design inspiration gallery will charm, amuse, and show you how design elements work together with color to make strong statements in large and small spaces. These gardens have the wow factor, the joyful, timeless sense of place that each person seeks and too few find whether the project is a blank slate or the redesign of an existing garden. Here are plenty of classic and modern ideas to draw on for inspiration in your personal process to create colorful gardens from the top down, year round. An old adage says that imitation is the sincerest form of flattery, so begin with a tour through some amazing gardens to find your kindred spirits.

Beautiful, exuberant beds use color and geometry to express the gardener's upbeat attitude in a rainbow of perennial and annual plants. By grouping shades together and allowing them to flow from the ground up, the design welcomes you to stroll, stoop, and sniff the flowers.

Designing with color

A TRULY WORKABLE DESIGN rests on the strength of basic elements and color to bring your vision to life in the garden. When you put these elements together to score your own personal garden symphony, it doesn't matter whether yours is a courtyard or an estate. Their harmony plays in every space and you can scale the plants down or up to echo good examples from either end of the spectrum. In illustrating each of these hallmarks and the effect different colors can have on it, this book puts the building blocks of the nonstop color garden in your hands. The strong establishing lines of a tall evergreen hedge in a public garden can translate into the dwarf version of that species to anchor your home landscape. A mixed hedge that includes flowering trees uses softer lines to set a cottage garden tone and a vignette of the same plants can create that same style in a bed next to your patio. Plant choices add seasonal color to the hedge line when you opt for shrubs with colorful new growth, fall color, or flowers. That combination of line and color takes the scene to a more prominent place in the nonstop color garden and gives you more pleasure in the doing.

Design Principles

A plant's overall shape, the geometric impression it makes, and the texture it displays constitutes its form in the garden. For example, no one can mistake the pyramid that is a spruce tree with the vase-shapes that characterize *Kerria* and mock orange (*Philadelphus*). Using form and color together, from the top of a tree's canopy to the groundcovers you choose, enables you to control the garden's flow and vistas. A lawn sets one kind of stage, a bed of vining Asiatic jasmine (*Trachelospermum*) or clumping lily turf (*Liriope*) quite another. Their forms

are flat, thick, and wavy, respectively, and your choice sets the table for the more soaring forms and colors.

The texture of a plant or a rock or a wall refers to how hard or soft it looks and is usually explained in relative terms between fine and coarse. The true design strength of texture and its ability to hold your attention often depends on color to be effective—a concrete patio is just a surface, but a blue slate patio has cool appeal and fine texture that garners attention every day, all year long. Because it is a relative term often seen in the eye of the beholder, you will find a variety of examples in this chapter and throughout the book. They are chosen to assist you in implementing colorful textures to establish focal points and to create views that work in every season.

The power of contrast grabs your attention like a gentle tap on the shoulder or a loud cymbal crash, depending on its colors. Coral bells (*Heuchera*) can offer shades from rose pink to orange and yellow to deep purple in sweetly scalloped leaves. A patch of any one contrasts well with upright green leaves, but a combination of coral bells' colors will strengthen an area's appeal in sometimes startling ways.

Variegation grows its own contrast; while bishop's weed (*Aegopodium*) is a neat groundcover plant, the white leaf edges of the variegated form deliver real pizazz. Emphasis in a design is sometimes measured by the viewer's reaction to one spectacular plant, like a spring-flowering tree when nothing else is in bloom. That can be achieved by using the power of color in contrast to everything else in that season or throughout the entire year.

Why does your eye sometimes zero in on a distant tree across the garden regardless of what is nearer to you? You simply see it, but the relationship between color

Color defines this long, narrow space and widens it visually; neatly kept evergreens repeat the clean lines of raised beds and a whimsical throw rug of lawn. Gray pavers create paths, a seating area, and water garden with contrast provided by bunches of color, among them blue salvia, white and yellow daisies, and pink hydrangea.

and size gives that tree its attractive quality. If the tree is in scale with the rest of the garden, it pleases the eye. Wise manipulation of scale lets you see each part of a design in harmony with the rest. It is the proper use of perspective in design that transforms a pasture into an intimate landscape or makes a zero lot line property feel spacious. Color aids perspective by allowing an element to recede or racing it into the forefront in support of the design. Gardens shown in Chapter 2 illustrate the ways to use scale and perspective, and Chapter 4 offers plants to achieve it with color in any growing zone. Sometimes a tree can appear farther away or closer than it really is, illustrating another function of design perspective, which is to manipulate space. In this book you'll find examples

of trees to frame a view and perennials to fill it, ways to create one vista by masking another, and see how color puts form front and center.

A focal point can be obvious, like a three-tiered gray fountain at the center of a deep blue water feature or a circular bed in the middle of a lawn made for seasonal annual color. You might fill it with brilliant gold violas topped with red tulips in spring followed by a dazzling display of tall, mixed-color zinnias in summer. Placement in the design determines where focal points will work best, and color puts the drama there to bolster their impact. Chapter 2 offers ways to find and create the focal points every garden needs and shows their impact in four seasons.

Harmony is a quality of balance, both in design and color, and works with focal point so the object of greatest interest can take center stage. These qualities create comfort, and while the balance and harmony of a design can shift through the year, they are essential. Without them, few views will offer satisfying emotional reactions for very long. Balanced garden scenes make sense visually but also geometrically regardless of their style or complexity. Even simplicity and variety in a design are not mutually exclusive if they are balanced. Think of "simple" as plain clean lines, clearly drawn forms with apparent texture, contrast, and clear proportions. But a cottage garden design can have all these qualities and still be wildly varied—raucous differences in flower shape and color within one vignette. Variety goes to the song among plants, ornaments, and hardscape within a planting that allows each to harmonize with the others and present a balanced view.

We'll take a timeless approach to garden design elements and offer modern strategies to use them, such as the idea of sequence as color across the seasons from top to bottom in the garden. Choreographing a year's worth of color, its sequence, is hard to do if you consider just one plant at a time. You will find the tools to take the macro view of powerful, unfolding color.

Using Color for Design Impact

Color matters in your garden because its presence or absence defines that space and distinguishes yours from all others. A garden design on paper comes to life when you choose its hues and put them to work expressing your desire for a color theme that spans the seasons

When a design is built around one tree, its beauty lies in symmetry and surprise. The contorted, deep-brown trunks of this maple combine rugged bark with elegant organic lines like arms on a candlestick. They are only outdone by the shocking orange fall foliage.

The power of line in design resonates in winter like in no other season. Upright and sturdy, vertical lines guide the eye and the soul to new heights even more when a garden is snow covered and bare of adornment.

or changes with them. *The Nonstop Garden Color* offers many ways to do just that using universal color principles and concepts. For example, as you will see, there are enough shades of any color to fill the year. Pink is no exception once you embrace its many variations. The pastel pink of flowering cherry trees and rose pink tulips in spring can lead to lush peachy shades in summer annuals like verbena and impatiens, with hot pink oleander and bougainvillea nearby. Fall's canna lilies can be a riot from peach to fuchsia, and a dusky pink paint on that potting shed ensures that your theme endures, even in a snowstorm. No matter what other colors you select as companions, your favorite color can reign; pink used this way invites a closer glance and sets a mood that is hopeful and contemplative.

How we see color is revealed by a study of simple physics, but the pleasure we take in seeing it in the garden is decidedly complex. Our experience of color is rooted in the associations we make to particular shades, and the memories and dreams they stir in us. Your earliest dearly treasured color memory may be the red and green of Christmas decorations. If those memories are pleasant, you likely gravitate toward red poinsettias, zinnias, and rhododendrons with abundant dark green leaves. On the other hand, if you much prefer the marching bands and flags of Independence Day, you'll temper that bold contrast by using shades of blue to cool the scene, with white and gold to diffuse red's impact. Neither approach is right or wrong, of course, but making the wrong approach for *you* can be costly. The information in this book is organized to guide you to the garden color palette that sings *your* song. Your palette will feel well-rounded when the colors are both diverse and compatible. On the color wheel that means using opposite and complementary colors in pleasing portions to achieve color balance. *The Nonstop Garden Color* moves from elegant examples of this balance to offer ways to measure your site's color quotient (or lack of one) with a color survey plan. By looking at your garden's color as it is presently, you can fashion a plan to fill in the gaps or recolor your world to better suit your style.

The power in determining a personal color palette and knowing which plants fit into it means you can translate the examples that inspire you. Finding the right color can be rather like the adage about kissing a lot of frogs to find a prince—you can go through many shades before you find the ones you really want around for the long haul. The keepers constitute your personal color palette that you will use to establish and reinforce your message. These colors are not limits by any means, but rather are the launch pad for your exploration of possibilities. To have four to six colors in mind when you plan and shop for the garden keeps your vision on track and ensures that each new addition will fit in. Even better is to know where each color pops and where more is needed, in a particular area or specific season.

Chapter 2 offers insights into color relationships and how they impact garden design elements. Its purpose is to inform the way you translate emotions into color, select shades to enhance your mood, and so communicate both to family and friends in three dimensions. You will find insights into the go-to color relationships you can count on to express the shades of emotion you feel. The use of color families further changes the impact of that design to set your personal tone. The absence of primary colors in a garden sets a more casual mood while their dominance demands attention as surely as a toddler. Line a perennial border with a mix of white and purple pansies, and you will draw eyes over them and into the planting, but choose pure yellow if you want to move attention down their length to the lilac tree beyond. This difference is universal far beyond the garden; one cannot imagine a set of pastel hazard cones on the highway, and few would embrace red as the only color in a room. You'll find innovative ways to put related colors front and center. Your choices and the resources in this book will shape a garden that grows where you live and pleases you from the top down year round.

Problem-solving with color

GARDENERS SHARE MANY CHALLENGES in bringing year-round color to the scene. The right color in the right place can address many issues, from improving a bland winter scene to keeping up with a garden bed in prominent view. By taking a look at common garden issues and ways to use color solution strategies to address them, you will step into the garden with a sharper, more optimistic attitude.

For example, as trees grow and shade increases in an area, it can become a green soup of leaves that is easily ignored. Flowers for shade may be few in some areas, but there are other options. Garden areas that are inherently dry or wet can offer colorful opportunities that enhance their natural beauty. When you bring color to difficult areas like these, the garden benefits and so does local wildlife. No matter where you live in USDA Zones 3 to 9, it can be a challenge to get satisfying color into the winter garden. But the plants that shine in winter deserve your attention for the drama they bring. The practice of "planting out" huge drifts of annual plants has gone the way of telephone booths, still around but few and far between. When a space needs color quickly and for months at a time, though, annuals still get the call, now in new applications. One of the most intriguing challenges is one that involves color palette, plant choice, and a keen appreciation of one's personal style: small gardens and small spaces within gardens. You'll hone your color skills and create sharp solutions in Chapter 3.

Stunning and practical, this pocket garden of color-rich succulents featuring *Sedum* and *Echeveria* provides clever living mulch to a difficult garden space. Wine and lime shades in thick, fleshy leaves are complemented by bright yellow variegation that lightens the mood.

Plants for nonstop color

GOOD EXAMPLES ARE ONLY pretty pipedreams without the specifics necessary to realize them where you live. The more than 100 plants profiled here represent the best color choices in trees, shrubs, vines, perennials, annuals, groundcovers, and bulbs. They are organized first by the color they bring and then by plant category with growing zone information that you can cross-reference with the USDA hardiness zone map in the Resources section. Brief growing notes are included but the emphasis here is on plants, both native and not, with excellent reputations for reliable growth and color in their zones. Of course, there are more plants you'll want to consider but this gallery meets these important tests:

- Plants compatible with a busy gardener's life
- Widely available in garden centers
- Seldom known to require much beyond routine maintenance

It can be difficult to say when plants that thrive across zone lines will deliver their color messages, so learning about them for your zone is important. The heart and soul of the nonstop color garden is the plants you choose and the pleasure you derive from them. The gallery in Chapter 4 offers options for different kinds of color in every season and inspiration to continue your exploration of colorful plants. From subtle shades to vibrant color statements, the plants included here come from and/or transpose into seasonal color options using illustrations shown in this book. With the gallery organized into color groups and appropriate zones, you'll find inspiration for every garden style and size. The plants are organized in groups associated by color impact: Reds, Pinks; Blues, Purples; Yellows, Oranges, Golds; Greens; Whites, Creams; and Grays, Browns, and Barks.

Flowering trees such as white dogwood offer design focal points for the spring garden. They shine more brightly when accompanied by a dazzling floor show of fuchsia azaleas and bicolored tulips. Opposites attract to bring color from the top down in simultaneous bloom.

How to use this book

IN *THE NONSTOP COLOR GARDEN*, you will expand your color horizons to embrace the real possibilities of year-round color and discover inspiring examples of what's possible to do in your own garden. Whether you are a beginning gardener or a veteran with years in the dirt, an avid do-it-yourselfer or someone working with a landscape architect on the garden of your dreams, this book will offer practical strategies for your success. When you want color for a new garden, need color solutions, or seek to enrich and personalize the colors in an existing landscape, the information included here can be your guide. If you think of garden color mostly in terms of bloom color, the ideas presented here will expand your color perspective. Tree barks, seedpods, and berries can also be featured players to display your colors across the garden and so carry your personal style themes through the year. The twenty-first-century American landscape brings together the best of classic design with the outdoor living concepts of the modern era. This book draws on both to offer great examples of color use in diverse gardens and to present design ideas brimming with color, practical tips and solutions you can use, as well as plants for every zone. You'll use *The Nonstop Garden Color* to inspire and inform your choices to enjoy color all year from the top down in your own garden.

Color harmony comes with repetition of shapes, even without similar shades to bring them together as when both weathered gray fence pickets and perfectly stacked lilac blossoms are sharply upright. The message is clearly optimistic and romantic, communicated by color.

Design inspiration gallery

ART IS, AT ITS HEART, a way of seeing something where nothing—or something else—exists. A sculptor sees a subtle figure in a solid block of rock, a photographer sees a clear view where others see chaos, and a writer sees ideas that become words.

Landscape architects and garden designers see a year full of color, texture, line, and all the design elements in one unfolding plan. They translate their visions into plants and hardscape in myriad different ways to interpret seasons, moods, and garden styles, as you will see in this gallery. Gardeners like to be inspired and sometimes can be downright copycats, with good reason: there are some views too lovely to be seen only once. It's perfectly acceptable to take good ideas home, even take photos or make sketches of them, and then transform them into your own. The next step comes with analysis—deciding what you like and why—then adapting those features into the reality of your garden. For example, a pure xeriscape or tropical design may not, per se, be appropriate in your climate, but its elements certainly can be and its mood will follow.

Whether it's small touches that refine your garden or the complete redo approach, you will find a catalyst here. When you explore a pleasing design, the math and geometry may be complex or minimalist, yet it's always coherent in its own way. The plants and colors fit together; their placement and hue has an inherent sense of rightness. You can find fabulous color everywhere, but the moods and styles of botanic gardens and residential landscapes offer a range of wildly diverse possibilities for your interpretation. This chapter offers excellent examples of public and private gardens, from east to west and north to south in all seasons. It will charm, amuse, and show you how design elements work together with color to make strong statements in large and small spaces. These gardens have the "wow" factor, that joyful, timeless sense of place that each person seeks and too few find whether the project is a blank slate or the redesign of an existing garden. Here are plenty of classic and modern ideas to draw on for inspiration in your personal process to create colorful gardens from the top down, year-round.

An old adage says that imitation is the sincerest form of flattery, so begin the path to your nonstop color garden with a tour through some amazing gardens. Rest assured—you'll find kindred spirits among them.

22

Spring

Spring garden design features the first colors and new growth of the season and makes space for annual flowers to bring their shades up close and personal. This inviting seating area sings of comfort and hospitality on a cool spring night.

When a spectacular flowering shrub, such as the *Rhododendron* genus, leads the spring show in a garden design, it is best accompanied by equally beautiful plants chosen for their compatible colors and bloom times.

To reflect the emotional hopes of the season, a spring garden design paints a scene of bright colors in new growth, brilliant blooms, and freshly painted benches. Details of every flower catch the eye of visitors, both humans and pollinators.

Summer

The design for a summer retreat puts the gardener above its colorful plantings for a great view. Its casual style makes a space for working in the garden and relaxing in private all summer.

Delightfully welcoming you from the street to the entrance,
this front garden reveals its maker's style and sets its mood.
The public space puts a face on the family who lives here with
friendly, cool colors on a summer day.

The summer garden offers a chance to bask in the sun with a riot of flower hues as warm as the season. To create a cooler, more calming mood, give green shades more prominence; up their profile with variegation and a mix of hues.

Fall

Below: In many areas, the arrival of fall shifts our focus back outdoors as temperatures moderate, and successful landscape designs reflect that. Such designs feature weatherproof walkways, raised beds, and a fall color palette in plants.

Right: In every garden style, consider how the scene shifts as colors come and go. Often the design includes ornaments in colors compatible with fall garden shades that create seasonal focal points.

Favorite fall colors and plants are as varied as geography, yet everyone appreciates their changing hues. From native plants to fall color annuals, this garden embraces golds, reds, purples, and every shade in between.

Winter

Winter colors don't have to be dull. A quiet, snowy day brings design strengths to the forefront with diverse, strong lines, bold forms, and gorgeous plant combinations that know no season in the Winter Garden at the Sir Harold Hillier Gardens in England.

Winter landscapes in areas of little or no frost are designed to feature the architecture of structures and plants, more than colors. When flowers are fewer, repetition of line and harmonious colors delivers a unified message.

Look closely at the garden in winter to see its colorful jewels: a berry here or a flower there. Perhaps because they are fewer, the garden's joys are all the more precious—to you as well as to birds and other wildlife seeking sustenance.

Designing with color

GARDEN DESIGNS ARE LIKE ORCHESTRA SCORES—both are usually complicated and first seen on paper, but are realized right before your eyes in living color. Each design element can be considered alone, yet all must work together as surely as violins and oboes must, or the composition fails. Line defines the vision, and form adds a third dimension to shape the scene. Texture illustrates the difference between reality and

A lark of a small garden space where the use of color is sure to incite smiles and invitations for a casual afternoon chat. The blue-lilac color palette on the washed boardwalk repeats in the plantings of blue and purple annuals and vines and keeps the scene cool on the hottest summer day.

appearances, while scale and proportion reinforce perspective and enable color to work. The concept of unity can be understood as the marriage of balance and focal point, much like the orchestra must coalesce for each solo to be appreciated.

Nowhere is color as powerful as when it drives emphasis, sequence, simplicity, variety, and contrast in the design. Because of their relative weight and importance, these elements as well as pure color, are addressed in this chapter. Color interprets the elements as you direct, from the simplest projects and plant choices to the most sophisticated materials and installations. To grasp how color can transform any one of them, it is essential to be aware of these basic principles of garden design.

Design principles

Line

Landscape design is universally acknowledged to be both art and science, and nowhere is that more readily apparent than in the use of line. You feel its effects as you instinctively follow a sidewalk, guided by its lines, yet its calculations are arithmetic. The landscape architect or garden designer must see a feature, such as a gently curving path, as a creative vision but must also be able to measure its arc and calculate area. Otherwise, there would be no way to accurately draw the walkway, or know how wide it will be, or know what can grow alongside it without overcrowding or looking sparse. Lines lead the eye in the garden and often determine where and how fast the feet walk through it.

Lines may be as narrow as a branch or as wide as a reflecting pool, and their arrangement may vary from style to style, with differing impacts. Looking across a wide lawn, for example, a line of trees across the way become a view you can walk past at any pace. But make that lawn longer than it is wide and it becomes a beeline, causing you to hurry along as if the trees might disappear before you can reach them. Classic water garden design begins with a strong upward line that flows from the surface skyward. The line may be a tree at a pond's edge, a clump of stately perennials along the west end to catch the sunset, or a fountain right in the middle. Soaring lines offer important and distinct contrast to the flat surface of the water to draw your gaze toward the sky and the heavens above, to appeal to your better angels. They are placed intentionally, as every line in the garden should be.

Without a diversity of lines, a garden would be a collection of plants with no point. But without color, lines are lost. Line uses color to attract or distract, to establish a constant or bring on a moment of instant gratification in the garden. You might want a bed that is edged neatly but that also looks as if it were part of the lawn below. You can achieve that by using the same color of greenery to reduce the impact of the line between them. But if it's a tree you want as an early spring focal point, make sure its colors fill its silhouette with shades that are in stark contrast to those nearby. In turn, a particular color may seem to almost embrace a line so as not to be overlooked on the garden palette. It's hard to ignore a trellised rose or a mailbox that seems to grow out of a clematis because the plant and its color have become the line and so a seasonal focal point.

The combined power of line and color in garden design draws stunning gray trunks against a winter's blue sky and lights up the spring with salmon and gold vase-shaped shrubs. The lines of a garden bench or patio may be quite utilitarian and geometric, even downright boring; the colors you select for plants, hardscape, and accessories are what make the scene bright and welcoming. In a garden bed, the straight lines of many annual and perennial plants deliver a neat message, but it is the colors and curvy petals of flowers like zinnia and daisy that touch your heart.

Straight or zigzagged, steeply S-curved or formed into long, winding paths, lines organize the garden, and those that are unchanging create design unity. Fencing, trellises, and gates are often made of dissimilar materials, but they can be used to unify and ground the design

Continued on page 42

Different kinds of lines can combine to feature the best of diversity without confusion when color guides them. Burgundy red and lime green use their narrow, curvy lines to soften the straight, brown lines of this entrance.

Nonstop color illustrated

STRUCTURES LIKE THE PERGOLA, steps, rocks, and gravel in this design establish visual interest and provide a destination in the garden. Such hardscape is permanent; differences in textures and colors offer contrasts in shape, surface features, and a variety of earth tones. Without colorful plants throughout the year, however, their inherent beauty might feel cold and distant. With them, the structural elements draw in the eye and the feet follow to explore the space.

SUMMER creates a cozy retreat with color. From the hammock to the roses on the pergola to coneflowers and phlox in the beds, red, purple, and pink warm the scene. The groundcover mondo grass, can be a year-round green carpet in some climates. Dwarf variegated shrubs, such as the abelia at the first step, set the stage with multicolored leaves in shades of green, white, and pink. Clumps of yellow cosmos and 'Autumn Joy' sedum bloom between the rocks to heighten the impact of both. Plants around pergola are mix of low evergreen shrubs, such dwarf yaupon, and mixed orange and yellow perennials, including daisies and daylilies. Tall conifers offer striking, dark green contrast to the shrubs, including dramatic oak-leaf hydrangea (*H. quercifolia*) with creamy white flowers above dwarf weigela shrubs with their variegated leaves.

FALL colors continue the theme, with seedpods adding additional earthy brown elements. Autumn crocus in patches along the steps and around the pergola add bright purple notes. Though the roses on the pergola are leafless, their striking dark gray vines remain. Oak-leaf hydrangea ages to reddish purple and a few dried flowers remain on the shrubs, adding a silvery sheen.

SPRING introduces the new, lighter-colored leaves of the abelia. Sedum and coreopsis have new leaves, too, in a light green. The blue iris and pink peony border the pergola, while the new green leaves and a few pink flowers on the roses lift the overall green effect. The oak-leaf hydrangea has light gray stems and new leaves. Weigela is covered in deep pink, trumpet-shaped flowers.

Continued from page 38

with the introduction of color. By emphasizing these diverse lines with a signature color, you mask their differences and plant your style flag year-round.

When particular garden lines appear only at times, seasonal color adds another dimension as an accent or focal point. The angular stems and twigs of osier dogwood emerging from a snowbank is exhilarating because its lines are red. In another season, a cloud of muhlygrass plumes is breathtaking because every line that draws them is cotton candy pink. A clumping groundcover like lily turf edges paths and fills low-profile beds until its purple bloom spikes draw you in with lines that feel like spring's birthday candles. That's when you really notice these plants and can choose to continue the strong lines and bold color choice elsewhere in the garden with tall, purple perennial salvias that maintain the same optimistic lines from summer to fall. The result is a seasonal accent followed by a seasonal focal point in one line/color combination. From top to bottom, a garden's lines define its limits and color helps you push them.

Form

Three-dimensional and dynamic, the garden design element called form refers to the shapes created in the landscape by nature and/or you. Each form—a slender column, fat orb, cascading fountain, or one of many others—carries its own message. The way they are used sets a mood and often evokes strong emotions. If you immediately like a designed space, it is most likely its forms and their colors that are pleasing to you, whether you realize it consciously or not. For example, an *allée* of trees with spring-flowering deciduous canopies feels light-hearted and carefree compared to the same design planted with muscular, evergreen pyramidal forms. Repetition of pyramid shapes is inspiring and perhaps humbling, whether executed in cedar trees or ancient stones, but its vibe is seldom described as friendly. Accompany that same pyramid form with complementary upright oval and vase shapes of similar height, and the same *allée* takes on a different mood entirely. To establish form is to set the essential cachet of the garden, to ground the design with visual elements that retain their essential silhouette over the seasons.

Form can be the most versatile of design elements, subject as it is to natural variety in organic forms as

Form draws three-dimensional shapes that define the landscape. Color makes them permanent and imposing, like this chunky boulder and peaked gazebo, but form can also be seasonal. From the rounded purple-leaf plum tree and leafy green trellis to spiky purple butterfly bush and Russian sage, summer forms speak.

well as human intervention in them. A rugged stone wall seems permanent, a hardscape element that will be in the garden forever. True and true, but which effect it will have depends on the wall's materials, form, and color. Carefully carved, ash gray granite blocks bear little resemblance to stacked yellow sandstone. They are equally beautiful, but the first has an air of formal elegance because its form has been evened and shaped by a person and its color is cool. The second wall will feel more casual since it remains in a more natural state with warmer colors.

By the same token, a big evergreen shrub may grow into a naturally rounded form and serve as an anchor plant to break up the rigid lines of a wooden fence. It is prized for its imposing presence and shiny leaves in wine bottle green. But in the hands of a skilled and loving topiary gardener, that same plant can become a surprisingly whimsical focal point form. Some would dismiss that notion as perverse, and the overall debate about the beauty of natural plant form versus the possible manipulations rages on as garden styles shift over time. There is a world of plants, materials, and color choices in between carefully manicured landscapes and completely naturalistic designs—find your style and use form to make it so.

The forms of plants, structures, hardscapes, and ornaments are essential to expressing mood in garden design, and color amplifies that effect. For example, form uses color to create or obscure views. An evergreen hedgerow can define an intimate mood with tall round, rectangular, or even boxy forms. It can be a sturdy, comforting backdrop to the summer border or serve as a baffle between the patio and the neighbors that increases your comfort zone. If the hedge also produces scads of carmine red berries, its friendly form becomes the winter view, too. In the same way, a small deciduous tree may have a spreading, weeping, or wildly loose silhouette and make you feel decidedly optimistic. But that form will bring more drama if shocking pink flowers appear early and its gray trunks form a neatly pruned centerpiece in a parterre or other quadrant design.

Form uses color to reinforce themes and plant the garden firmly in its environment. When the woods behind your house erupt with rich shades of golds, reds, oranges, and purples in fall, even errant limbs and lumpy shapes can be heartwarming. The same explosive, joyful colors can be found in trees and shrubs with similar natural forms for the home landscape. Thickets and large, upright profiles will set a bittersweet autumn mood and enlarge the garden's footprint by echoing the world around it.

Form establishes silhouettes and profiles, and color maximizes their effect. That's why it is important to recognize which forms in a planting will show off their colors simultaneously to avoid a visual train wreck where neither form nor color can be appreciated. Even a "crazy quilt" pattern positions each square carefully to show its best advantage, and so it should be in garden designs meant to be viewed at close range. For example, a collection of small shrubs might line your well-traveled front walk. If they are exuberant vase shapes, their grace may be obscured in a monochrome color palette. Give the form its due with color, and let chartreuse sit next to pea green followed by variegated leaves of cream and dark green. Equally effective is an arrangement that allows pink, yellow, and red flowers to bloom at the same time on quite different forms. You might include ovals with some that cascade out of the bed in places, and because their colors harmonize, each silhouette becomes a featured player in the arrangement.

Texture

While lines are easy to see and forms demand attention, texture is a more ethereal landscape design element. A line may be straightforward or complex, and forms can be monumental or delicately small, but both are clearly just what they seem to be. Texture, though, is *perceived* as much as it is *seen*, and your comprehension of it depends on the relativity of one kind to the others. To understand texture can be a real mind-bender as it requires you to see what you feel. If you find the touch of silk to be soft, lustrous, and oddly delicate, you can imagine that a fine-textured plant would feel the same way if it actually felt like it looks. Its tactile reality may be quite different: perhaps fine, threadlike leaves are actually sharp to the touch. You can think of texture in any medium. Consider curly hair—some people have long locks with shiny ringlets the size of your thumb, others have tightly wound, little wiry springs close to the scalp. It matters not whether the hair is actually soft or crisp with styling gel; different kinds of curls are defined by their visual relationships to one another. The ringlets look distinct, with

Combining elements of differing materials creates textural diversity. Its colors draw interest and set the tone where desired, as with this formal entrance. The stark contrast of the black gate to the gray wall would be utilitarian at best, but for the softer texture of the evergreen vine that bids you welcome.

clarity and visual weight, when compared to tight curls that meld together into one shape and so appear finer in texture. Look at fabrics, furniture, or architecture for your own metaphor, but know that if the coarser texture is also darker in color, the difference becomes clearer.

Fine texture in plants derives primarily from leaf size, shape, and arrangement, sometimes assisted by the form that delivers them into view. Deeply cut and papery leaves that flutter easily, small leaves so thin you can see through them, cascades of diminutive compound leaflets, willowy leaves and those covered in tiny scales—these are the classic vehicles of fine texture. They occur in every color imaginable but are most associated with lighter shades, including pastels, because they stir similar feelings of quiet confidence. Fine texture can be obvious, like a frilly fern, or less so when it occurs seasonally in a cloud of tiny flowers. Once you recognize and feel its appeal, you will see it everywhere in sharp contrast to the textures nearby.

Coarse texture is the visual opposite of fine texture. Sometimes this quality comes from gargantuan leaves, massive trunks, and flowers with big petals that often overlap. In other designs, the coarsest quality will be found in the bulky silhouettes of boulders and plant groups that look heavy even if the individuals are not. But here the devil is in the color details since the same leaf will deliver coarser texture in richer shades and

Continued on page 48

Nonstop color illustrated

WHAT A WONDERFUL WAY to dress up a seating area or patio! The colors lead from season to season in a seamless parade. The proportions are so good that even the smallest purple flower gets noticed as much as the purple wall above it. The area between these buildings could easily be visually dead, an overcrowded mess, or a lot of little plants with no relationship to their surroundings—but this fluid, colorful, eye-catching view is in perfect proportion to its space.

SPRING colors are pinks, from pale and ethereal to brightly raucous, and several shades of purple. These colors are achieved primarily with early-blooming annuals such as foxgloves, snapdragons, pansies, and petunias. Indian hawthorn offers bouquets of pink flowers tinged in white and durable evergreen holly shrubs put on tiny white flowers. The crisp white flowers of doublefile viburnum (*V. plicatum*) really stand out; their blooms are but one element of this signature shrub's three seasons of color.

SUMMER builds on the pinks and purples of spring with the addition of red. Roses maintain a strong pink theme, while holly and camellia leaves are shiny dark green. The viburnums put on striking red berries as bright as the roses. The spring annuals at the lowest height have been replaced by similar color mounds of purple fan flower, red geranium, and sweet alyssum in lavender and white. Taller plants include blue salvias alongside scarlet red and shocking-pink zinnias and cleomes. Tree roses add a snap of white flowers.

WINTER moves into greens and red-purples. Evergreen Indian hawthorns add dark green foliage with slight red tinges in winter. The dark green hollies past the trees, before the rose trellis and bench, sport winter red berries. The camellias between the benches show off their red flowers (though camellias are available in many colors). It's fine to add color using "outside" elements, such as bows, wreaths, ornaments, and lights. The homeowner brings in brilliant color and seasonal excitement by surrounding the seating area with white Christmas lights. Although the rose is now leafless, its red hips add color. The doublefile viburnum, also leafless in most climates, will have purple-black berries and, in the Deep South, burnished red leaves.

Continued from page 45

wide variegated patterns. For example, the broad sword-shaped leaves and dense clumps of a perennial such as a hosta display coarse texture in solid green hues. However, hosta varieties with fat stripes or what look like globs of white paint decorating the leaves will be in-your-face-coarse next to the others. In the same way, surfaces that are sharply drawn, netted, and waffled with distinct veins can further heighten a leaf's coarseness when they also employ strong colors.

Perhaps the least understood and poorly defined texture is the medium range. It is easy to say that medium texture is anything not fine or coarse, and many plant descriptions certainly do so. The mid-range is distinct and, while not necessarily inherently showy, can sometimes be transformed by color.

You may enjoy the vibrant red and purple of new growth on a shrub with smallish leaves, such as loropetalum. The leaves do not change their texture whether they stay purple or turn green, but when combined with different colors of leaves or flowers, they can be bullies or friends. Medium-textured green leaves set the stage and keep it fresh, no matter what else goes on in the planting—that's why they are so frequently employed. The same plant colored purple will stand out, perhaps *too* much, and compete or overwhelm the others. Medium texture also has a different impact depending on its gloss, much like wall paint and lipstick do.

Texture as a design element plays right into color's wheelhouse and goes hand in hand with it to accomplish desired effects. Perhaps nowhere is this more apparent than in designs that feature particular plant groups, such as drought-tolerant or tropical plants. No matter how much you love these plants, without differences in texture provided by color, these gardens can look painfully monotonous.

Cover the walkway with pavers or mulch in deep red-brown shades to add color texture that winds its way through desert plants. And use the evergreen of tall cacti

---

Even though this design features green, green, and more green, the rich variety of textures sets each plant apart from the next and the result is far from boring. The bright wood and pavers provide additional breaks in the color and texture.

with maroon manzanita trunks to keep color there in the off-season. In the tropical garden, beds full of cannas bring bold texture with dense sword-shaped leaves, but they take on a life of their own when variegated leaves mix with the solid greens to highlight their texture and emphasize each plant's silhouette, creating a deeper, more interesting view.

Scale and Proportion

A classic adage reminds us that beauty is in the eye of the beholder. Or, to paraphrase what a Supreme Court justice once said about pornography, "You know it when you see it." So it is with the landscape design concept of scale and proportion. The reality is that a landscape design professional spends weeks ensuring that every part of a landscape is designed to suit the scale of the site and that each part of a garden is in healthy proportion to the rest. When it works, you may not be aware of scale and proportion at all—the garden just makes you feel welcome.

What you notice most often is what *doesn't* work—when something in the design seems out of whack. Sometimes the error is obvious, such as a brightly painted wall that looms over everything else or a fountain that is clearly too small for the huge water feature around it. A neutral shade of paint can make that wall disappear, but a new fountain installation may need a new budget to correct the design problem. But other mistakes in scale and proportion seem intangible as when parts of the garden blur together without distinction or a tree stands out oddly, like Gulliver among the Lilliputians. For elements in the landscape to work together, each must be in proportion to the others; to get that agreement is a mathematical exercise furthered by the wise use of color.

By definition, scale and proportion are the same concept: they describe the relationship of elements to one another. But in gardeners' terms, they are often separated for ease of understanding and application.

Unity gives a sense of coherence to every garden design, and the color palette of even the smallest space can deliver the concept wholeheartedly. The variegated hosta stands out here, yet it unifies the scene by repeating both the white of the pickets and the yellow-green of the groundcover. The ornament reflects their colors, further uniting them.

The idea of *scale* most often applies to the property as a whole, the macro view, while *proportion* refers to what lies within one view in the garden, the micro scene. This may seem like a distinction without a difference, but it's a practical way of looking at and planning for a pleasing landscape. The things you can see from a bird's-eye view affect scale: structures, hardscapes, relationships between cultivated beds and lawn to utility areas, path and porch dimensions, mature tree heights across the property, and similar concerns. Proportion focuses on the plants and features within the design, especially as they relate to one another within the same view.

Unless you start with a blank slate, you usually cannot entirely control scale, but you *can* control the proportions within the garden. To do so means selecting what you plant and how you maintain it with the other plants in mind, whether you planted them or not. Should you remove a big tree to let in more sunlight, or will that throw the entire back half of the garden out of proportion? Installations big and small count here, too, from retaining walls to bird feeders—a swimming pool would be nice, but is there room for it both physically and visually? Proportions also change with time and, much like you can let the hem out of most skirts, you can usually adapt.

Some changes can be foreseen, like how much plants will grow or when it might be time to dispense with the sandbox and swing set in favor of a perennial border. A well-proportioned garden bed design considers the relative heights and shapes of plants as well as their color impact. Its overall size should not dwarf whatever is nearby nor be too small, like an afterthought. Geometry and arithmetic can set exact proportions, and color makes it work by adding emphasis here and reducing it there to maintain them. For example, if three-quarters of the spring flowers in a bed are the same shade, the view will be a monochrome blur. No amount of attention to their heights and flower shapes will matter if different shades and colors are left out; proportion can be established with color diversity. When you put in a new bed designed to be primarily trees and shrubs, and take into consideration their mature sizes, the immediate results can be jarring to your sense of proportion. The bare areas between new plants loom large and blank, even with ample mulch. To start with larger plants is not always a wise option, but planning ahead can be.

A large and imposing garden structure makes a brilliant focal point but can appear to float in space if it's not grounded by plants. Together with thematic color choices, they can achieve a harmonious balance, as when the tranquility of this shady seating area is ensured in shades of green.

Consider the scenario for a possible perennial border: you can overplant the new bed, knowing you will transplant half in a few years. The proportions in the new bed can be established with faster-growing perennials and woody plants that can possibly form the basis of another new bed in the future.

Perhaps the most glaring example of proportion failure seen every day is a big tree with shrubs and perennials planted too close to its base. No doubt it looked right at the time, but today the tree has a fat ring of green and flowers around its base that makes it look oddly unstable, as if it might choke on them. The plants that were supposed to embellish the tree's beauty instead create a loss of proportion. Fortunately, by moving or enlarging the bed, this problem is readily solved. And if you take the opportunity to echo the tree's flower or fruit colors in the bed below, so much the better for a focused view.

Unity

Like being comfortable in your own skin, unity offers an intrinsic peace to the landscape without ego. That is, a unified garden carries one message without ever being heavy-handed or overdesigned. You create unity when you make the fundamental decisions about your garden's overarching style and carry that imprimatur throughout the property all year. Perhaps your unifying scheme will be formal paths and plantings or a loose collection of beds and seating areas. A formal style with brick paths and planters by the front door deserves tree mirrors—the dramatic trunks, bark, and fall colors of the centerpiece front yard tree are reflected in those chosen for the back and side yards. An informal style may snake its paths around the property from the front door to the back fence, encompassing sun and shade, flat and sloping spaces. Yet you can establish unity in the shapes of the paths as well as mulching materials and flower colors in every plant group.

Unity is the thread that sews an entire garden together into one tapestry. You set its pattern with plans for cottage garden plants or a formal parterre, a naturalized landscape or privacy hedges with plenty of fall berries. For example, your cottage garden might focus on pink, yellow, and white flowers, whimsical yard art, and picket fencing. It is easy to see how using the flower colors in

Continued on page 56

EXAMPLE C

Nonstop color illustrated

THE THREE-SEASON PALETTE for this lovely view uses purples, reds, bronzes, golds, and greens. Here, color unites a home landscape with an intrinsic feeling of peace and calm. A unified garden carries one message, and it's the thread that knits an entire garden together. Formal paths and plantings maintain and repeat key design elements, such as straight lines, curves, and forms to establish unity; the colors establish mood. Essential, too, is the addition of color in container plantings; even shrubs and trees can be grown in large, colorful pots.

SUMMER colors set the tone for the other three seasons. The groundcover bugle flower (*Ajuga*) lines the walk with deep purples with some green and brown variegation in small, leafy rosettes. To the right, another groundcover like coral bells (*Heuchera* × 'Golden Zebra') displays multicolored round leaves in yellows, golds, apricots, and bronzy reds. A dogwood tree (*Cornus*) on the left provides a major focal point, sporting light green leaves in contrast to darker shades at the rear and red maples (*Acer rubrum*) to the right of the house. Fine-textured ornamental grasses (*Miscanthus*) and sturdy purple-leaf loropetalum echo the tree colors. Dwarf spirea shrubs bring accent colors to eye level in containers.

FALL deepens the red tones in the groundcover bed, colorful red berries appear at the branch tips on the dogwood, and the loropetalum maintains some red fringe flowers. In bold contrast, white plumes on fountain grass *Miscanthus* are eye-catching, and, in the pots, spireas display golden yellow fall foliage.

SPRING shows off the lighter colors of new growth, brightening the mood. Bugle flower blooms with pale blue spiky flowers, and the new growth of coral bells is a subtle combination of green, yellow, and apricot. The dogwood tree blooms bright white, matched by the rhododendron's trumpet flowers. Red maple leaves are crimson red, the ornamental grasses are spring green, loropetalum shrubs bloom with fresh red flowers, and pots of spirea burst with new celery-green leaves.

Continued from page 53

the hardscape and ornament will unify the setting. Or the deep evergreens of a huge hedgerow down the side of your house might be repeated by small hedges beside the front door and around the patio out back.

A garden's mood is tied directly to unity and is expressed by your personal take on the garden's best uses. A design that starts with your desire to entertain outdoors year round will be unified by different elements and colors than a design meant to create a family's retreat from the world. Both settings will need outdoor living/cooking areas but call for very different materials to suit the mood. An outdoor kitchen and seating for 12 can set a formal mood in wrought iron or carry a more casual message with wooden benches and tables. The serenity of your personal oasis may speak out from slick, clean surfaces, cool colors in the blue-gray range, and repetition of upright plant forms. Using similar colors and basic forms contributes to unity while a random collection will feel painfully chaotic regardless of the gardener's intentions.

The repetition of key design elements—straight lines, exaggerated forms, and bright color contrasts, to name a few examples—can establish unity and sing your mood year-round. The house and garden structures are a big part of this aspect of unity because they carry design statements and color across the seasons with their constant presence. The scale of the structure to its surroundings aids unity, as does its most dominant lines. The front garden is the establishing view for the entire property and most often the place where unity is found or lost. A ranch style house is essentially a rectangle with matching windows; it would look out of sync with ornate columns framing the front door. Equally jarring might be a rank of pyramidal shrubs taller than the windows. A more conventional foundation planting could better unify the scene. A house that is multistoried will have more upright lines than the ranch style and can visually support a larger front garden. Without that larger apron, the house looms and sticks out like the proverbial sore thumb. With it, the upright lines and colors of the house can be repeated and interpreted in plants and hardscape. It is a conscious unifying decision to see

---

This brilliantly colorful container planting shows essential design elements in an elegant capsule. Each color on the pot is echoed by the plants in it but drawn with lines and forms in ideal contrast. The result is a unified focal point that fits perfectly in its setting.

The serenity of this patio comes from the use of balance to create a peaceful mood with a mixture of textures. From fluffy, rounded hostas and lush vines to sharply drawn iris leaves and pavers, the view engages and calms its visitors.

windowpane shapes reflected in walkways and steps, to echo the colors of shutters and chimneys in stone planters and retaining walls.

In this last example, it is equally vital to unity for colors to be established that set your mood. If a deep green lawn carpet is your pleasure for the front garden, finding places for lighter and contrasting shades in accent plants will create an elegant, thoughtful mood. If you like a lawn but also want a tropical tone, your plant choices and colors will be bolder yet still bring unity because you use them together to tell your story. These strategies and thought processes also apply to other structures in the garden such as a gazebo or potting shed, just on a more intimate scale.

Balance and Focal Point
BALANCE

Just as a good story has a beginning, a middle, and often many plot twists before the end, but only one plot, so your unified garden will tell your tale from front to back. While unity considers the entire picture created by your design, balance and focal point draw a finer point on landscape relationships. Both depend on comparing—balance measures the differences between elements while focal point calculates the impact of one over the others.

The question of balance in a landscape design goes to the sense of place, the ethereal yet essential quality that makes a garden truly distinctive. You see it in the visual weight of objects and plants, and often in the relationships between their colors. The sense of place separates your garden and your color choices from all others. Balance can be found within a pot, a garden bed, or entire landscapes; it imparts reassurance and certainty. It brings a sense of internal harmony, a confidence that there is a steady hand guiding the garden in a specific, colorful direction. That is the essence of why generations of humans have found peace in the garden, and why we still aspire to it.

Like all elements in design, this one derives from a combination of geometry and emotion. Mathematically, there are formulas to determine how much plant material will fit in a given space. Following those calculations, roughly equal materials on each side of an axis will achieve physical balance. The delightful wild card in this equation is how design uses balance to create surprises, to leave room for the unexpected. You might create a hidden view or choreograph a rainbow of blooms that progress through the garden, and balance allows those scenes to be seen. Balance works because it allows visitors to compare and contrast plants and garden features. Without it, the affect is flat and nothing stands out, regardless of your attention to color. The lack of balance is off-putting and may explain why visitors do not return—the experience makes them feel out of kilter because the math is wrong.

But complete numeric balance seldom satisfies the eye or the soul. When you walk into a garden that is too perfect and symmetrical, you may feel your spine stiffen, and you probably will not linger. If the point is to hurry you along, as through a commercial complex, overbalance wields power. Neither extreme contributes

---

This focal-point seating area uses color from the top down to be certain no one misses this destination. Using a blue-purple palette, the design creates a rustic trellis with purple color pops that lead the eye and the body to the comfortable chairs and chaise.

to a warm sense of place. Embracing both the concept and reality of balance enables your imagination for plants, ornaments, and color to soar without chaotic results. Balance maintains perspective and allows for its manipulation, as when you want to make a space seem larger than it is or feel more intimate. With it, a garden feels confident and inhabited; it resonates with your taste and color palette. Without it, a garden lacks focus at best and, at worst, is downright disconcerting.

FOCAL POINT

Focal point success depends on the overall balance and unity in a design achieved through the wise use of the other elements. Two of the most important lines in the landscape are those that define its axis, the point around which all else in the design revolves. This intersection is the first focal point in the design, the place your eye will naturally go in a cohesive design. The axis lines are drawn in the air, so to speak, in that they are clear, but not usually interpreted literally. One may run from the big tree in the front yard through the house and terminate at the back gate. The other might skew from the garage to the farthest back corner. Where they meet may be in the center of the space, or it might not, but that spot is sweet and can focus all your other efforts. When you see a design on paper, the axis should be clearly delineated. If your garden is already planted and the axis lines are not obvious, it will behoove you to find or establish these lifelines to design harmony. Focal point and color go hand-in-hand, since the focal point can go dull without color to make it sing.

There are at least two sorts of focal points you can employ in a color-focused garden. In practical terms, one can be called *sustainable* and the other *seasonal*. The first is a focal point you will see every day and build a view around. To find it, make your own mini-axis: stand at your back door (or window), look into the space, and take a photo. Then go into the space, find a place you can or would like to sit—this can be anywhere so long as you can see that same point. Take another photo from there, compare the two to see where they come together, and that's the focal point you will be able to sustain over your life in the garden. This is the place to plant your flag—to make your garden style statement with something you want to see daily. A sustainable focal point might be a seating area, a statue, a bird-feeding station,

A well-balanced seasonal design offers attractive color combinations at every level in the scene. A spring-green lawn gives way to blue-green daffodil clumps topped by their white and yellow flower hues. They cozy up to the exhilarating sight of pink-and-white-blooming saucer magnolia.

or a tree. This is also the place to establish your signature color. Seasonal focal points are dramatic—a spectacular flowering tree, a shrub with unmatched fall color, and winter features that call you out to see them. They are singularly unmatched for impact in their season and always depend on color for their power.

You are the color conductor of a very personal orchestra that can respond with gorgeous, nonstop impact in your garden year-round. Each design element is a tool in your kit; all will be profoundly affected by the colors you choose for them because hues transform impacts of plants, ornament, and hardscape.

Understanding color concepts

THE WAY COLOR CAN TRANSFORM a design depends as much on math as on building trust in your own perceptions. As it is with the basic elements of design, so it is with color in the landscape—part art and part science. We can measure its hue and depth relative to other colors, but we have not yet created a gauge to calculate emotional responses. That is why although bright red is the attention-grabbing color of traffic signals, it is also the country's favorite color in flowers—red roses, geraniums, and poinsettias far outsell all the other colors available combined. We react to that color in different ways, but with red the reaction is always strong and quick whether it's your foot on the brake pedal or a heart-felt smooch. It is also why much plant breeding is done for color, such as deeper shades in fall leaves, more and brighter colors for summer annuals, and barks with richer tones that are revealed in natural peeling. The principles of color and the concepts they bring with them to the garden are simultaneously universal and very personal. The same is true of the ways we can translate them into color from the top down and year-round.

Color Principles

Color is both a physical matter and an ethereal concept because what you see and how it makes you feel are both brain-based. Light is composed of electromagnetic radiation organized into wavelengths. When your eye perceives color, it physically captures light and translates it into the colors you see, the visible spectrum of ROYGBIV (red, orange, yellow, green, blue, indigo, violet). These seven colors correspond to the seven notes in a musical scale in that they relate to one another in incremental steps. Within each color, as within musical scale notes, there are well-defined tones and hues that

the human senses transform in individual and sometimes quirky ways. Black and white are also a matter of physics in that black is the absence of light and therefore color; white is the presence of all colors at once.

As early as 1666, Sir Isaac Newton organized the colors into a circle known as the color wheel, which has been used ever since in every field of art because of its simple clarity. Many iterations have been drawn, from simple pie shapes to shaded panels displaying hues in order of their intensity to intricate overlapping shade colorations. All color wheels are based on the primary colors—red, blue, and yellow—represented in three equal segments to underline their equivalent status. These are the three pigments that cannot be created by mixing others and, conversely, all other colors can be made from some combination of the primaries. The power of red, blue, and yellow is their clarity and bold simplicity. In their purest form, primary colors are impossible to ignore.

The color wheel can show secondary colors by cutting the classic pie into six slices. These are the colors that arise from combining the primary colors directly with the one that lies next door on the wheel. Red mixes with blue to form purple, so it is depicted between them. Blue and yellow turn into green; therefore, green follows blue and precedes yellow on the color wheel. Yellow combined with red creates orange, which sits between them to fill the sixth piece of the pie. By bisecting the color wheel yet again, the hues known as tertiary colors can fit nicely between the colors that give rise to them. Their names explain their parentage and are usually hyphenated: red-purple, blue-purple, blue-green, yellow-green, yellow-orange, and red-orange. These names are purely descriptive and have other, more subjective monikers,

Cool brick and shutter colors warm up quickly when accompanied by plants in deeper hues of lime and purple. Turn up the visual temperature and warm the welcome even more by adding eye-catching red and orange tones.

such as violet for red-purple and indigo for blue-purple. The wheel lays out in graphic fashion both the colors and their relationships to provide a reference point and a launch pad for using them.

Color and Emotion

Emotions are triggered by color because the brain stores previous reactions to it, mostly individual but also in pathways that are universal. For example, you may have seen a red rose and reacted positively to its bold, bright color long before anyone ever sent you a dozen to woo you with their charms. Even without a personal connection, color has the power to evoke oddly similar emotions in people of widely diverse experience. Anyone, anywhere has only to read of Wordsworth's daffodils to ache for their yellow glory. Thousands have travelled from other continents to where Wordsworth lived in the Lake District for the experience that puts color and emotion together so dramatically.

These universally felt reactions to particular colors are well understood, and while there are cultural variances, the nonverbal messages are the same.

- **Red** and its partner **pink** stir the passions of love and war. While red is extreme and can be violent, pink is unconditional and devoted; they are two sides of the same coin.
- **Orange** brings out both optimistic and engaging emotions and sends messages related to its shade. Darker oranges, such as terra cotta and pumpkin, have earthy associations, unlike pure orange and lighter hues that give you more serene feelings.

- **Yellow** can be mellow gold or bright as a canary's feathers and makes you feel certain and confident. Yellow is associated with creative ideas and cool intellect, but can also make you feel impatient, as when others' ideas are not in sync with yours.
- **Green** feels balanced, which may be why we garden—to gain that balance.
- **Blue** is the only color with a mood named for it, an existential sadness oddly coupled with resilience and even hope. Perhaps that is why it evokes loyalty in people, too, and has names like navy and royal blue.
- **Indigo** and **violet** are the two faces of purple; the former is closer to blue and the latter borders on red

When the primary color in a design is green, its diverse shades and hues bring that scene to life and raise its emotional impact. The result is a comfortable, harmonious unity.

at times. They inspire feelings of intuitive intimacy and personal self-confidence.
- **White**, the presence of all colors of light at once, brings feelings of formality, expansiveness, and peace; **cream** evokes a more naturalistic feeling and may be cool or warm, depending on its hue.
- **Black** is the symbolic and practical opposite of white. It works as a startling contrast as brown does for cream.

Color relationships

Color and Garden Harmony

The color wheel is like a map in that, while you are not obligated to take all the roads at once, it is wise to know the options available. But it is also like a musical score—the colors, like notes, must harmonize to be pleasing, much less memorable. Whether duet or symphony, in music and color harmony comes from the symbiotic arrangement of the parts, when the combination is more than the sum of its parts. At first glance and upon deeper examination, harmony communicates a feeling of inherent calm and order. Lack of harmony feels too bland because nothing is eye-catching and you find it unnecessary to get involved. On the flip side, disharmony evokes chaos, and you do not want to engage the scene. Either way, the result is that you hurry past, vowing to achieve more balance and harmony in your own garden.

There are several ways to achieve garden harmony based on color wheel relationship. Any three colors are said to be analogous when they occupy adjoining space on the 12-part wheel, such as red-orange, red, and red-purple. Most of the time, one color dominates and its hues and shades are used more extensively than those of the other establishing colors. Complementary colors stand exactly opposite each other on the color wheel. They can be counted on for stable, bold contrast, an important element in color harmony. Both hold equal presence in the garden; shades and hues of each one are employed to extend the complementary palette.

Because a garden changes every day, it's wise to take the long view of color harmony. This concept is dynamic, ever changing over weeks, seasons, and years, yet your interpretation of it is timeless. Equally timeless and incredibly personal are the tweaks of obsession, the color details with deep meanings, if only to you. Perhaps there is no shade that will satisfy you like the turquoise sky in a Georgia O'Keefe painting. Or you might prefer the neon aquamarine of an antique beer sign, a similar but very different color in fact and in emotion. Set aside the rules and seize the shade that lights you up and let it ignite the color fire in your garden.

Color Vignettes

The successful harmonious melding of design strength with color elevates both. To take harmony from a great concept to beautiful reality means coloring the basic design elements cohesively. Nonstop garden color creates an inspiring view when basic design elements compose a scene with a physical balance of repetition and contrast. The repetition brings the comfort of familiarity, but can also lull one into a stupor. Contrast can be jolting, for good or ill, but a good balance of repetition and contrast inspires unity and holds your interest. Their harmony is an overarching concern, beyond one choice or another, and explains why you want color in your garden at every level in every season, from groundcovers to the tallest trees.

Design elements are the arrows in your quiver, ready to be deployed. To organize your thoughts, think of the potential views as color vignettes and select plants that work together to fulfill the elements. Color across the seasons comes from vignettes planted for sequential color. Any size space can contain a four-season bed or border, and smaller properties gain focus from their use.

Vignettes are essentially garden views of intimate or grand scale, and while you do not want to see the same sight everywhere, shared components promote harmony. The vignette should be built around a template that can be repeated for unity yet allows room for plenty

of variation. Some are three-part designs, essentially triangles of complementary colors or taken from the three elements of classic floral arrangements—straight, soaring lines of inspiration, others bent to brush the earth, and filler shapes that tie them together. Formal style vignettes rely on color and geometry to establish scale and proportion, while more abstract templates are less constrained and may use subtler shades to maintain perspective. Hardscapes and ornaments within such a four-season bed or border can and should play featured roles, but the gardener's heart will beat faster when most

Left: Blue, green, and gray conspire to calm even the wildest mood in this sheltered spot. Slate-colored shades in the wash of the planter boxes give way to lighter tones in the ornament and hosta, and then even to the well-ordered aggregate and stones below.

Below: A riot of color brightens any space—as well as your disposition. Buttery yellow and citrus orange establish a sunny mood, accentuated by the use of their color opposite, royal purple.

of the color derives from plants. Green, gray, and cream are often anchor colors that appear in every vignette and pair well with most other colors; when repeated, these colors become unifying elements. Here are possible combinations for sequencing plants and emphasizing color groups. Each plant in these top-down color vignettes is included in this book and *you* will expand on them.

- A heartwarming, passionate color ensemble begins with red and includes pink, coral, and salmon as primary color players. Imagine a tall tree canopy on fire in spring with native red maple (*Acer*) and in fall when blackgum (*Nyssa*) goes red. Joining them in later spring can be buckeye (*Aesculus*) and from spring to fall, Japanese maple (*Acer*) hoists the red flag for months. Step down with long-blooming, pink-flowering spireas (*Spiraea*) that also provide yellow fall color. Use more yellow for contrast in witch hazel (*Hamamelis*) followed by kerria (*Kerria*) shrubs; mix them with red-leaf barberries (*Berberis*) and evergreen shrubs such as hollies with red winter

berries (*Ilex*). Fill in at ground level with bearberry (*Arctostaphylos*) and punch up spring with cottage pinks (*Dianthus*) and summer astilbes (*Astilbe*). You might use this vignette over and again with variations along the back fence or in pairs to establish a front yard garden.

- Purple joins blue, violet, and lilac to set a cool, serene mood. Their sophistication increases with deepening hues. Put the focus on shrubs with the pure purple of Oregon grape holly berries (*Mahonia*) and winter color. It will provide tall yellow flower spikes in spring and bold texture all year. Add classic color with Meyer's lilac (*Syringa*) and light blue, effusive Ceanothus for spring and summer blooms. Make room for strong lines in here with beautyberry's (*Callicarpa*) arching branches dotted

Diverse but equally rich, the combination of color shapes in flowers make this crowded scene harmonious and inspiring. This offbeat, highly personal cottage style design imparts casual confidence and the balance of pink, purple, and green carries that message well.

---

with metallic purple berry clusters in fall. Bolster summer color with chaste tree (*Vitex*) and rose of Sharon (*Hibiscus*) in blue and purple hues, but find space for white varieties of both for pleasing contrast. Accent the vignette with clumps of perennial Salvia to add every color in this group and punctuate this level with variegated leaves or other perennials of equal color weight such as daisies (*Leucanthemum*) or great globe thistle (*Echinops*). Lay in carpet bugle (*Ajuga*) for light blue spring flowers and purple leaves all year.

- The earth tones—yellow, orange, terra cotta, and ginger—feel whimsical as a group, appealing as they do to your sunny side. They can dominate a perennial bed or border with a complementary set as contrast. Start at ground level with the patterned orange leaves of coral bells (*Heuchera*) and the yellow-green of moneywort (*Lysimachia*) to run the table with these colors for months. Accents of variegated lily turf (*Liriope*) and *Pachysandra* can contribute very different greens to add interest at the groundcover level. Pick a variety of heights and shapes of perennials, such as black-eyed Susans, daylilies, and tickseeds (*Rudbeckia, Hemerocallis, Coreopsis*, respectively), but repeat two or three across the planting for continuity. Interplant them with compatible species that expand the months of color provided by the primary plants. For accents in the blue-purple complement, select speedwell (*Veronica*) and irises for spring, and gayfeather (*Liatris*) and Joe-pye weed (*Eupatorium*) for late summer and fall. Vary the height with shrubs like fragrant sumac (*Rhus*) for burnt orange in summer, repeated in the fall color of 'Mt. Airy' *Fothergilla* and carried into spring by pink mountain laurel (*Kalmia*) plus red- or salmon-flowering quince (*Chaenomeles*).

Color in place means using every plant part and growth stage to best advantage in one view. To create this kind of vignette, you can expand the idea of bedding out. The updated view adds other plant groups that take on the same color focus through the year. For example, a shrub bed of Edward Goucher *Abelias* brings enchanting vase-shaped thickets. The spring growth is coppery red and in summer turns bright green with coppery overtones, some very pronounced. The shrubs are topped with clusters of pinky-white trumpets for months, and then those leaves deepen their red hues in fall. Such plants retain interest in winter with graceful clumps of gray stems. Add a small flowering tree such as star magnolia (*Magnolia stellata*) or harlequin glorybower (*Clerodendrum*) to raise white or pink to the next level, and/or surround the shrubs with low-growers like lamb's ears (*Stachys*) or perennial *Sedum*. This vignette is built around one plant with four-season interest with other plants that echo your color at different visual levels.

But other plants above it or beyond it in the design can also be incorporated and reinforce scale, too. A huge spreading tree at the center of the view, such as *Catalpa* or golden raintree (*Koelreuteria*) makes a powerful focal point. Use those colors again, but not in a bed beneath the tree—put that creamy white or yellow and salmon in a circular bed along the axis between your house and the tree or in a bed off the deck in view of the tree. You might use knotweed (*Persicaria*) and ornamental grasses with a Catalpa to take its creamy white colors into summer, fall, and winter. Or plant blanket flower (*Gallardia*) and cinquefoil (*Potentilla*) to complement the raintree. Color becomes form and line as you use it this way to establish a color profile and sightlines in the garden.

The idea of creating a garden scene using fewer plant groups can be especially useful in shady spaces. For multiseason good looks, you might cast actors such as texture, contrasting greens, and variegation. Hardy ferns, wake robin (*Trillium*), and hosta set the perennial stage beneath whatever is shading the area. You can add shades from a huge viburnum hedge (white flowers or purple fruits) or sassafras thicket (orange fall color) to the vignette in summer annuals and bulbs. Remember the mantra of repeating vignettes for top-down color all year: repetition for unity and contrast for interest.

Nonstop color illustrated

BALANCE GOES TO A SENSE OF PLACE, of internal harmony, and inspires confidence that there is a steady hand guiding the garden in a specific, colorful direction. In this three-season garden, there is balance on each axis in the tall lime-green pot that serves as a focal point. This wild and crazy collection of plants does not look calculated, yet it feels serene because of balance. The lawn serves as an accent in all seasons.

SUMMER sets the stage with a deep orange pot holding a mixed planting of diverse colors, as well as textures and heights such as bamboo, red canna lily, peach begonia, and a yellow-green sweet potato vine. More contrast balances the scene—among furniture, pots, and their plants as well as between the bright colors of the patio and more subtle hues at the rear of the garden. A deep lime-green pot holds ornamental grass with brick-red-tinged leaves and bottlebrush-shaped plumes (*Pennisetum* 'Burgundy Bunny'). A rich blue pot shouts with orange while a lighter lime pot contains 'Black Magic' elephant ear, deep purple leaves with lime-green veins. The columnar holly draws attention across the garden with boldly variegated leaves.

FALL highlights seasonal colors in a big way and anticipates the holiday season well. Pumpkins set the theme; both pots and hardscape hold shades of orange in flowers, gourds, and decorative lights. Ready to be noticed, witch hazel (*Hamamelis*) puts on brilliant fall color in apricot-gold-red-bronze. Ornamental grass plumes are plentiful, the holly has bright red berries, and the fire pit gets plenty of use.

SPRING colors keep the warm tones in this design feature, adding purple and white in bright, crisp pops to equal the brilliant colors of the containers. Bulbs are everywhere and balance the impact of the patio and the emerging new growth of trees and shrubs. Daffodils, crocus, and tulips echo the colors in witch hazel's golden-yellow blooms and the red osier dogwood's prominent red stems.

Color for maximum garden impact

Emotion, Value, and Intensity of Color

The way you use hues and shades together lets color set a harmonious tone in your garden. It is this interplay that shows the shades of your emotion as surely as it features the shades of color. Highly personal emotions are imprinted along with words and deeds into the color psyche of every gardener, and that is why certain colors satisfy us more when we translate them into the garden's plants and accessories. For example, Girl Scout green is very different from avocado green, and if one pleases you, the other probably does not. The first shade may make you recall your childhood or your favorite Irish bar, and if those are pleasant memories, you are not likely to be satisfied by a lawn that is less than pure grass green. But if you are a fan of the yellow-greens, it might stem from a love for Army jeeps, retro appliances, or the guacamole you hope to make when your tree produces. In the garden, you would likely embrace walkable groundcovers and pea gravel mulches without ever missing the traditional lawn.

This attitude of conscious engagement in choosing colors can impel you to look differently at plants and take no space for granted if placing color there can touch your emotions. It's important to remember that when a color causes you to react, your body responds as surely as your heart. Whether it's a stop sign or buckeye tree (*Aesculus*) in bloom, red warms just as the cool blues of a swimming pool flanked by butterfly bushes drops your temperature before you ever dive in.

These emotional responses to color translate to the garden in terms of value and intensity. These factors give you control over the nuances in the way color is perceived and so over the emotions you stir in the garden. They are also why gardeners and designers carry a fistful of color chips to the garden center—each shade has a story. Value tells you how light or dark a color is and sometimes reflects its emotional impact in the garden. Darker shades of the same color are considered to be of lower value than lighter shades. For example, burgundy red has lower value than cardinal red and evokes more thoughtful, resolute emotions. Sky blue is higher in value than cobalt blue. It is also regarded as more optimistic and lightens your mood, while low-value cobalt feels mysterious.

In the garden, value becomes a practical matter. Low-value colors fade from view sooner at twilight and appear after those of high value at dawn. At other times of day, visibility may depend on the distance between you and the planting, but is still related to value. Size matters here, too, since tiny pale pink flowers (high value) will be less visible at the same distance than tiny red ones (low value). This knowledge can inform your choice of which flowering plants to combine in order to express emotion effectively. It also explains why you will be wise to match one high-value plant with three of low value in a bed that is viewed early or late in the day. Conversely, in a full-sun-at-high-noon planting, the ratio is reversed, especially if the individual flowers in question are small.

Intensity measures the brightness of a color (as it does of light) and is highest when any one hue stands alone. This factor enables a long row of bald cypress

---

Any group of plants can fill a space, but colorful choices make the most of its potential to create a view. This color palette of blue, red, and purple stands up under scrutiny against the earth-toned background. Let deep blue dominate, balanced by white and silver stems and flowers in fewer numbers.

trees (*Taxodium*) to be a dark green, eerie presence yet allows you to see the same design planted in a different, single color in an equal but opposite way. For instance, a long row of avocado-green and then golden Ginkgo trees feels warmly welcoming but no less intense. You can very successfully use single colors for standalone, high-intensity focal points, such as a gazebo painted purple or, for a strong seasonal contrast, a hedge that has red berries in fall.

Intensity and its emotional message are tempered rather dramatically by using the color's shades, complements, and/or gray, white, or black. For example, if pink and white dwarf sasanquas (*Camellia*) join the red berries on a holly (*Ilex*) hedge, the scene seems friendlier and softer, even though all the leaves are stiff shiny evergreens. But imagine the hedge with its complement colors instead—perhaps found in redleaf loropetalum and bunchberry, a groundcover dogwood (*Cornus*). Now the message is steadfast, and you feel sure-footed just seeing red and reinforcing purple-reds.

After all, most emotions are gradations of three essential human feelings—love, hate, and indifference. In much the same way, most colors are gradations of hues that fall between the three primary colors of red, yellow, and blue. Gardeners employ shades of varying intensities and values to successfully interpret design elements into a diversity of emotions. You can begin with any color, but to ignore these important factors sends a flat message and inspires only ennui.

None but the hardest heart will be untouched by the hot jewels of summer color in the peach, pink, and red flowers in this grouping. The dark fence makes a perfect backdrop for flowers as diverse as round yarrows and zinnia, flighty white guara, and peachy hot pokers.

Top-down color

TO COLOR YOUR GARDEN from the top down to the ground all year can seem daunting without a plan. With pad in hand, paper or virtual, survey the colors you have and the ones you want.

Every property has immutable colors to consider first, the plants, structures, and natural features whose colors you do not control. You must decide how to deal with them, to incorporate them into your palette or to consciously mask them. For example, if you chose the site because the garden backs up to a native woods with dazzling fall color, the garden's sense of place naturally puts colors into your palette. Note the red or gold shades that you want to repeat in the fall below the tree canopy and/or in other seasons to reinforce them. Conversely, if the trees are evergreen or promptly deciduous, your

A call-and-response color pairing resounds from rooftop to driveway and beyond. A roof with red tiles, white walls, and a red-and-white awning holds forth, softened just enough by fence and flowers in more muted shades of the same palette.

full palette comes into play. Begin with spring-flowering and colorful fall trees slightly smaller than the background and then plan each lower level to emphasize one or more of your colors in each season. For example, the yellow flowers and autumn leaves of tulip poplar tree (*Liriodendron*) can be reinforced by *Forsythia* in spring and carried into summer with St. John's wort (*Hypericum*) shrubs.

When you inherit an existing garden, its colors also affect your palette. If it is rife with sunny yellow and shocking pink flowering plants, keep in mind that subtler shades of the same color will tone it down. If nuance is not in your emotional wheelhouse, choose equally strong but different colors such as purple and orange to diversify the color scene. When the garden is fully planted at one level—say there are plenty of shrubs—your colors can contrast from the perennial bed, where colors are usually longer lasting, and from small trees with dramatic form. In this way, the plants and their placement will bolster what's already there and stand out on their own. Thematic white gardens, for example, may not be your cup of tea, but if you've inherited one, you can shift the emphasis using your chosen colors. If a border features plants like white candytuft, add a companion such as blue Stokes' asters to liven up spring. Then take your blue palette into summer, perhaps with a collection of blue pots filled with annual flowers to keep your color front and center. Or if a bank of white hydrangeas dominates in June, add reblooming blue hydrangeas for summer color in a similar form.

Many homes have only a lawn, a few trees, and some shrubs when you begin to inject your palette into them year-round. These may be the easiest to assess for color and offer the most opportunities to introduce your personal palette. In such an ideal situation, if your home is gray with cherry red shutters, you might begin with planters painted a darker burgundy flanking the front door, perhaps planted with red geraniums. That might lead to adding a redleaf loropetalum (*Loropetalum*) shrub hedge, a holly tree (*Ilex*) for red berries, and the red twigs of red osier dogwood (*Cornus*). In this simple scenario you have used your signature color and its related hues through the garden all year. At this point, you can expand your palette to add in more colors, to enhance but not blunt your impact.

You may have a favorite color, as well as one you detest. That knowledge should be a guidepost in your color palette and inform plant choices for nonstop color. A word of caution, however, against the cavalier rejection of an entire color suite: White dogwood (*Cornus*) blossoms stand out against their own leaves but can shine even more when yellows and pinks or corals set them off. The supporting players from your color ensemble in this spring scene might include daffodils (*Narcissus*) below, and saucer magnolia (*M. soulangeana*) and pink Japanese snowbell (*Styrax*) alongside. But if you hate pink, you'll find coral-flowering quince (*Chaenomeles*), 'Einstein' daffodils with their coral cups, and the hardiest, coppery coral bells (*Heuchera*) will also work.

Your palette only works when you choose plants that will grow, of course. There are subtleties within zones, and local microclimates vary, but you will be well served to start with USDA hardiness zones and consult other resources. Those might include your state's Cooperative Extension Service for weather and soil profiles and maps such as those drawn for heat zones and for specific geographies in Florida and the West Coast. They will help you further define conditions and thus find suitable plants, but perhaps the best local resource is *you*. Keep your camera handy to record what you like in local gardens; shoot vertically to focus your attention on top-down color. Find a friendly horticulturist at the local garden center, attend garden expos, locate plant societies and Master Gardener groups in your region. They know what grows where you live.

With design elements and their impacts in mind, you can use your color palette to create new vignettes or refashion existing plantings. At times, however, your knowledge of color can do much more to meet the challenges of creating a top down, year round garden. Color can solve problems, as you will see in the next chapter.

Planning for top-down color makes beautiful, practical sense in a design that shades the porch from summer to fall in burgundy red maple leaves and that features terraces to frame the stairs. Seasonal echoes in the same color palette are found in the hydrangea and a variety of colors from caladium bulbs.

shady strategies
xeriscape solutions
winter interest
annual flower power
small-space challenges

Problem-solving with color

ON A GOOD DAY, a garden inspires feelings of peace and excitement simultaneously. There is harmony in the display, sometimes humor, but never boredom. When it's not right, you can feel it, but its shortcomings can also be measured and solved. Sometimes you see the problem in a garden design right away. Maybe there's too much of one color at one time or there's nothing to look at for weeks or months. A simple analysis, such as a weekly photo diary, will reveal colors and/or their lack and often offer clues to workable solutions. Other times, the plan and its plants surprise you when they simply do not work together or you discover that the setting itself is the issue. When plants do not physically grow as expected, review their needs and your care regimes. Timely pruning, fertilizer, and watering practices may get them back on track and return the colors you planned. The colors in your palette can offer strategies for shady and xeriscape settings, add winter interest from the top down, provide seasonal color, and keep small spaces interesting. Whether it's a tweak or a complete redo of the colors in a garden space, these options will assist in your decision-making.

Color solves the dilemma of transitioning from pond bank to garden by featuring woody plants with multiseason interest. Deep wine foliage near the pond and a frame of starkly contrasting green and yellow set off the focal point of scarlet red and draw your interest across the path.

Shady strategies

SHADE OFFERS WELCOMING RESPITE with a delicious air of mystery when done right. That shade may be inherited but when the trees you plant do grow and shade encroaches, your colors need not fade away. Interesting shade is all about contrast between colors, values, and intensities, but also between shapes and materials. As beautiful as a grassy green carpet can be, and despite the fact that it is often a unifying reflection of the colors around it, shade is not the place for turf grass. Where less than half a day of full sun shines, give in to the colors and contrasting forms of groundcovers to carry your color palette through the year.

Few other spaces can feature the green color suite as magnificently as shade does when it relieves a monochrome scene. Even a group of plants with essentially the same leaf shape can create a memorable view when their colors vary within this classic hue. Think of the sword shapes of perennial hosta, cast iron plant (*Aspidistra*), and canna lily (*Canna*) painted in blue-green, forest green, and bright spring green. When the tree canopy is low and dark green, consider the yellow-ish green leaves in shrubs around the edge. A row of 'Chardonnay Pearls' (*Deutzia*) or a small spirea shrub (*Spiraea*) will clearly define the area with color best seen in a mass of the same leaf shapes. Evergreen understory trees and shrubs can also maintain strong green all year. If they are missing from shade, add them but choose carefully for diversity of color and form.

Where more than indirect light is available, color-ful variegation and flowers can jazz up the shade year round or seasonally. Shrubs and perennials that have painted leaves bring their own clarity; many favorite plants in genera like *Hydrangea* and *Iris* have variegated forms. Where there is not enough sunlight for them to

Dappled sun provides enough light to sustain lawn grass but leaves cooling shade that can be enhanced by pastel plant colors, light stone hues, and fine-textured, medium-green leaves.

Above: Designing to incorporate various elements in a shady setting can be a challenge. The judicious use of ornaments for focus and detail works well with a diversity of green colors and plant textures to lead the eye deep into this very personal retreat.

Left: A shaded entryway can be overlooked by visitors or have little pleasing visual impact beyond its architecture. Using color such as that found in these hydrangea shrubs can solve this problem in one plant with multiseason interest.

bloom, their forms and colors carry the day. Or you might choose hues from the tree canopy's fall colors to carry color into the shade in other seasons. Where red leaves dominate autumn above, echo it in shrubs like burning bush (*Euonymus*) that have or will develop similar leaf colors, plus red violas, red kale, and ornamental cabbages. Keep the accents red with tulips for spring and red spider lilies in late summer. Add a garden gnome with a tall red hat for more emphasis.

Even one stunning plant chosen for texture and color can change the dull shade below tall walls or endless evergreen hedges. Imagine a dwarf Japanese maple tree

The definitive line of a long garden border can be maintained in shade if a major edging plant makes the transition and displays a brighter green than the plants around it. Thick, hardy clumps of bright green fern fronds lead the way even as leafy trees above deepen the shade.

and a large gray rock surrounded by painted ferns and coral bells (*Heuchera*) punctuating the shade with color for much of the year. In winter the branches and twigs of the maple will glow gray, its fine-textured silhouette in harmony with that big stone accent.

Adding texture and palette colors to shade through hardscape or ornament can be your best friend. Consider a path to break up the shade and add color; use slate in a blue palette or concrete pavers painted white to catch more light. Focus on a place to sit—a table and chairs or a bench—with texture that stands out. Sleek metal surfaces set a contemporary mood yet sit well with gray tree trunks and contrast naturally with greens and other colors. That same shady retreat done with wooden furnishings will feel more timeless, especially if the path is covered in cocoa-brown mulch.

This cheerful, welcoming design uses the same variegated hosta plants in shade and part sun, where they bloom joyously and attract bees. Under the leafy tree canopy, leaf variegation is their best feature.

Where water runs through shady places, you have the grand opportunity to color the swale with rocks of different sizes and shapes. Use the smallest sizes that will not float away in the lowest level and step up to sizeable

Staggered gray pavers form the perfect floor for this shady short path and the design makes clever use of an otherwise lost space. The primarily green scene is enhanced by pastel flower colors and variegation.

flat rocks (perfect for butterflies to sun on) and boulders where there is room. Their profiles create height and form plus flat surfaces and crevices where light plays in wet and dry times. The rocks act as colorful mulch, too, and prevent erosion.

Where no slope or natural flow exists, think about installing a water garden to transform the shade environment. Bubbling water appeals to the eyes and ears equally and creates a sense of tranquility that can be therapeutic in a noisy world. The shade garden may be set apart from the rest of the property and is often in the backyard. That makes it the perfect space to express your most whimsical ideas, to surprise visitors and sometimes yourself. Where plant heights are too consistent, all tall trees and low-growing perennials, and where shade is dark and dense, add architectural elements: columns, posts, or poles painted in your signature shade. Use them as plant stands or trellises with strings of clothesline wire between them for vines to grow on. When the vines are leafless, hang twinkling lights or chains of prayer flags from one to another. If you want to hang a giant wind chime or build a tree house, shade can be the place—just keep your color palette handy.

Even an edible landscape design needs shade—to sit in, if not to grow in. A beamed pergola provides sturdy support for grape vines and a restful space beneath, where darker greens dominate and soothe. The ingenious path of continuous pavers through lawn and gravel expresses a colorful style and points the traveler's way through.

Xeriscape solutions

THE DEFINITION OF XERISCAPE GARDENING is deceptively simple: to select and grow plants that thrive with no additional water beyond what is available from rainfall and runoff. It is often depicted in desert climate designs but it is actually a method and style of gardening that can be used *everywhere*. Although the approach is minimalist at times, water-wise design is no reason to forsake color.

Xeriscape is a radical idea, yet one that makes superb sense. To rely primarily on rainfall can be strategy that adjusts to changing environmental conditions. Some areas of the nation have experienced a decrease in annual rainfall as average annual temperatures have steadily warmed in recent years. There and elsewhere, gardeners are irrigating less to conserve water and lower utility bills. Plants that cannot adapt can stop blooming or succumb altogether to the changing conditions. The

situation may seem dire, but it presents an opportunity for smart new installations or redesigns that incorporate color in different ways.

Natives to the Rescue

A staple of xeriscape is the increased incorporation of native plants into designs; its grand benefit is color with a sense of place. A stately oak or elegant birch (*Quercus, Betula*) sends a message of homegrown beauty. Similarly, a stand of bright yellow tickseed or the pink daisy shapes of purple coneflower (*Coreopsis, Echinacea*) looks and feels natural even though it was planted intentionally. When a nonnative tree or big shrub dies, grind out the roots and reuse the remaining hole by filling it with soil from elsewhere in the garden, mixed with other organic matters commonly used in your area. Then add a native that fits your palette plan. As with any new planting, it takes time for natives to put down roots and develop their superior innate tolerances for local conditions. Sometimes that means providing water in reservoir bags or with low-pressure drip irrigation systems. Some soil amendment in previously occupied soils and regular use

Left: The play of sun and shade shifts the subtle colors of boulders in this xeriscape. Accents of fine texture and upright lines in shades of green and darker brown give over the focal point to the tan-and-gray palette.

Right: The use of color to define space and highlight its use can be especially important in low-water landscapes to keep the message clear. Here, gray stonework and a timber pergola combine with the rich greens of living mulch in a minimalist plant design that makes this corner shine.

of a light organic mulch improves transplant conditions here as everywhere. Such investments pay off in the long run with faster growth, and more and stronger colors. To choose a native replacement in an existing planting, consider the color palette you have created and which to emphasize going forward. If blue and purple colors have been prominent, there are native berried shrubs aplenty from the pinky-purple to dark blue-black—and that's only the viburnums.

While native species have always had a place in the modern American landscape, in many cases they have been superseded by exotic (or nonnative) plants. Well-adapted exotics are chosen for outstanding features including brilliant colors or just because their "foreign-ness" appeals; their numbers increase each year. You can count on them to perform as well as any native in their zones. For example, it is hard to imagine gardens without the Asian natives Korean stewartia (*Stewartia*) and crape myrtle trees (*Lagerstroemia*).

Fortunately, native species plus their selections and cultivars are more available every year thanks to increasing appreciation of their rugged qualities. You may have seen native yellow witch hazel (*Hamamelis*) or creamy oak leaf hydrangea (*Hydrangea*) on a hike and marveled at their flowers. But if the species is too large for your garden, there are now smaller cultivars with neater habits and the same, if not better, colors.

Designing with Natives and Nonnatives

Designing with native and well-adapted nonnative plants together is a grand way to harness their color and energy in keeping with xeriscape sensibility. You have no doubt heard the phrase "right plant, right place," and

Color diversity in plant leaves transforms what might be lost space in a dry-side garden into a ground-floor organic mosaic. Steely blue-gray and claret red stand out as focal points amid ground-hugging greens.

Round and spiky shapes distinguish the cacti in this xeriscape design, which uses blue and gray pebble mulch to maintain, add color to, and visually cool this sunny, dry site.

this strategy demands it. Find out how much rainfall your area has and note differences in your own microclimate that might be due to runoff. Then select plants to suit the conditions. This may be as simple as noting the best performers already in your garden—or perhaps the neighbor's garden. Investigate the origins of nonnative plants that are new to you, and if they hail from an area similar to yours, put them on your list.

Your garden can boast nonstop color without draining the lake or your pocketbook for excessive irrigation. A good place to start is to reconsider thirsty turf grass lawns. Replacing all or part of yours with hardy groundcovers creates a sustainable and often more colorful alternative. Where it is impractical to add plants to a changing situation, hardscape can reduce water needs and reinforce your colors. If you want a patio, deck, or outdoor kitchen, this is the place for it. Hard surfaces are a blank canvas, so use them to reinforce passionate rose-red or stunning Caribbean blue from your palette. Color pavers and walls in your primary shade, and then add ornaments and furnishings for contrasting values and companion colors too. Where plants are established but color and space are lacking, let hardscape carry the day—and your colors—into a harmonious combined design.

Colorful plant materials can flow like a living stream through landscape designs for dry gardens. Mixing colors, textures, and plant forms from round to crawling and trailing defines this succulent planting.

Winter interest

GARDEN COLOR NEED NOT take a holiday when the days go from brisk to bracing to frozen. In fact, a unified and balanced design must embrace winter interest features or be unsatisfying. This dilemma is readily avoided with smart plant choices and combinations that carry your message through the dark months.

There are three prime winter views in a property of average size. First should be a colorful sight that welcomes you home. Second is one visible at close range from your favorite window. Third is a view you have to look out into the garden to see, usually near the far point of the landscape. While the first and second views might be trees or shrubs accented with bulbs and ornament, the third view is the province of evergreen and deciduous trees as big as scale allows. The big trees you plant are a legacy, ultimately an investment in a garden's future. Luckily, many trunks develop colors, patterns, and habits

early on that only improve with age. If you want to add bold winter color and strong silhouettes to be seen at a distance, choose one large evergreen and one large deciduous tree.

Evergreen trees offer strong form, brilliant color, and captivating barks easily recognized from an acre away. The dark red-brown shaggy barks of red cedar (*Juniperus*), dawn redwood (*Metasequoia*), and bald cypress (*Taxodium*) establish a muscular profile. Their presence implies stability, defines the space, and softens the harsh winter mood.

Lots of winter color in every part of the garden comes from the barks of deciduous trees because they peel, strip, and ravel to reveal glowing inner shades. Included in this group are Japanese zelkova and crape myrtle (*Lagerstroemia*); between them lies every shade of toasty tan and cinnamon brown. Some trees create patchwork patterns as pieces fall away, as on lacebark elm (*Ulnus*) and sycamore (*Platanus*). Other trees, including river birch (*Betula*), hold their peeled layers in curly ribbons while a few, such as smoketree (*Cotinus*), discard bark in thin flakes.

In planting this important third view, consider how well the color and geometry of ridges and furrows work at a distance. For example, the lightly ridged gray bark of oak trees (*Quercus*) displays subtle texture up close but looks solid gray-brown at a distance. Austrian white pine (*Pinus*) combines that same gray with white into bark that looks distinctly like puzzle pieces even across the yard. Sweetgum (*Liquidambar*) has dark brown ridges with surprising symmetry, but for a gnarly and

---

Red berries are a classic source of bright, cheerful color during the winter months.

unforgettable look from farther away, look at the deep cocoa of golden raintree (*Koelreuteria*).

Color Pops: Berries and More

Winter color and often wildlife amusement come in colorful berries and drupes that persist well past the solstice. If you have not had the pleasure of watching birds devour them on an icy morning, it's not just the berry colors you are missing in that view from your favorite window. Viburnums offer the widest range of berry colors in diverse shades of dark, bright, and pinky reds, as well as blue-purples and almost ebony. They are often seen against burnished red and purple leaves that are among the last to fall. Blackhaw viburnum holds its fruits well for an especially long time, deep purple in tiny grapelike clusters. Evergreen Japanese ligustrum has fat clusters of purple berries, too, that can look brushed with white powder. The holly (*Ilex*) family is perhaps the most reliable for glossy red berries in sizes from knee-high to 30 feet and more tall. Holly forms range from squared off hedges to single trees that serve as focal points; evergreen and deciduous, alone or with company, there's a holly to fit every view. Dogwoods (*Cornus*) bear beautiful scarlet red drupes in clusters. These seed packages may be small and oval-shaped or large, round, and dramatic as with the Kousa dogwood. Equally beautiful red orbs can be found on strawberry tree (*Arbutus*), decorating stunning mahogany limbs. The most celebrated shrub for winter garden color must be red osier dogwood. Its bare stems are as shiny red and alluring as a vamp's nail polish. Where summers are not too hot, grow it.

Plan for bulbs to surround a focal point statue, line a path, or surround the patio to plant color where you want it for winter. As autumn leaves turn, coral-red spider lilies (*Lycoris*) and golden autumn crocus (*Colchicum*) echo the transition color palette at ground level. Plant them alongside the late winter bulbs, which can begin to bloom in January or just weeks later. The canary yellow of winter aconite (*Eranthis*) and crisp white snowdrops (*Galanthus* or *Leucojum*) lead the parade, followed by purple and white snow crocus (*Crocus*) and early yellow daffodils (*Narcissus*). Grape hyacinth (*Muscari*) delivers navy blue flowers while wood squill (*Scilla siberica*) glistens in Wedgewood blue. Their optimism is just the cure for late winter blahs, and they start the year's color show from the ground up.

Designing a garden that grabs the eye in winter puts the colors of the season at wonderful odds with one another. Blue sky and white snow blanket a prairie garden on a blustery day, made even more beautiful by clusters of mahogany-colored seedheads on leafless stalks and huge sheaves of tall grasses gone tan.

Annual flower power

THE FIRST FLOWERS that many people tend are often annuals because they are easy to grow and can reward with unparalleled colors quickly. Two seed packets and a patch of sunny soil soon becomes a row of bright yellow marigolds in front of a tall patch of rainbow zinnias. Seasoned gardeners may think annual flowers are too easy, a distraction from other, more majestic plants. They might seem like unnecessary fluff because each is so short lived when compared to other plant groups. But annual flowers are there every year to deliver cheery, reliable, relentless color. Their unequalled range of hues enables you to put color where you want it, at almost any level of the garden—even in baskets hanging from ropes thrown over tree limbs. There's little or no waiting for annual color, and with just minimal maintenance, such instant gratification can be yours for months. Seed catalogs and garden center racks can be intoxicating, so the wise gardener approaches both with a plan already in mind.

Annuals seldom need an audition to play diverse roles in the nonstop color garden. They can carry your colors through the garden from wherever they are established into closer view. Where forsythias and tulip poplar (*Liriodendron*) set a yellow and gold theme, annuals like pot marigold (*Calendula*) and snapdragon (*Antirrhinum*) can fill beds while black-eyed Susan vine climbs a lamp post. Their yellow shades will unify the garden scene, and you can add to their appeal with similar shaped flowers in different colors: round pink gerbera daisies (*Gerbera*) and blue china asters (*Callistephus*), pink stock (*Matthiola*) and purple annual salvias.

This plant group can be the bridge that takes spring colors through summer or they can anticipate the fall shades to come. If your fall focal point is the stunning reds and burgundy of black gum tree (*Nyssa*) and viburnum shrubs, be sure annuals like deep red-purple amaranths (*Amaranthus*) are included for summer. Some have upright flower spikes, but the long chains of

Left: A difficult site, such as this one defined by chubby, light gray boulders in a mix of sun and shade, can be tackled by using annual flowers for pops of color. Here, their presence personalizes the space, their roots do not compete with the tree, and their colors are a pleasant surprise.

Right: Hardscapes and evergreen plants define this mixed border of annual and perennial flowers. While gray pavers, dense green tree canopies, and perennial clumps such as iris and gayfeather do not change year to year, annuals can and will change, as you desire, leaving you with a possibly changing color palette.

love-lies-bleeding (*Amaranthus*) are plush and dramatic. Combine them with the bold green and burgundy patterns of coleus (*Solenostemon*) and pink cosmos.

Annuals can be more than an echo of your color palette; these flowers can shout it. In films, the "establishing shot" sets the mood for the entire production. So it can be in your annual plantings when you use them to cue visitors for what will come in other seasons with similar forms as well as colors. Perhaps you wait all year for the distinct petals of white dogwood (*Cornus*) and cascades of white spirea (*Spiraea*) flowers that cover the round shrubs each spring. You can highlight their importance with the pinwheels of flowering tobacco (*Nicotiana*) and Madagascar periwinkle (*Vinca*) along with thick white stands of sweet alyssum (*Lobularia*) and tall annual delphiniums.

In a garden otherwise devoted to pastels and evergreens, annuals can be a wild contrast yet stay within the color range you have established. They can continue the heart and soul of those colors in brighter, bolder hues. When light pink spring roses greet spring with the equally precious petals of saucer magnolias, annuals pick up the thread with intensity: the bubble-gum pink of verbena, hot pink phlox, fuchsia petunia, and rose mallow (*Lavatera*). These darker shades of deeper value can stand up to the summer sun and glow against the solid greens. Combine the deep pinks with light green Canterbury bells (*Campanula*) and gold California poppies (*Eschscholzia*), and punctuate the scene with striking white daisies (*Osterospermum* or *Bellis*).

Texture Changes Mood

You can use bold-textured annuals to embellish the color palette and change the garden mood entirely to suit the season. For example, the rich orange of paddle-shaped petals of Hibiscus pair well with the huge upright red

---

The addition of annual flowers to a formal walled planting design lightens its mood immediately and allows for almost-instant color in any season. Their colors will seamlessly enrich and reinforce any theme established in perennials and shrubbery. Bright orange gives this scene an extra pop.

A memorable, pollinator-rich design puts annual flowers along the edges of beds containing roses and other flowering shrubs. This "yellow brick road" of nectar-rich flowers leads visitors to the gazebo, but not in a way that makes them hurry.

Abyssinian banana (*Ensete*) and the refreshing green hearts of elephant ears (*Alocasia*, *Colocasia*). Together they instantly transform the corner of your deck into an oasis of tropical color and texture. Or you might choose fine-textured annuals to draw the eye into beds around trees with brilliant contrast. Such a group might include pouty diascias, softly lobed monkey flower (*Mimulus*), prim columbine (*Aquilegia*), and velvety painted tongue (*Salpiglossis*). Their colors can paint a rainbow that is no more than knee high and amazingly diverse.

Annual flowers planted en masse move people. Bright red salvias can lead the way down the path to a shady grotto or surround your front door and reinforce its colors. A bed of tall pink and white or rose *Cleome* waves hello and lures visitors from across the garden. They can fill a bed in heights from 6 inches to 6 feet with easy-to-grow textures that repeat and extend your color palette. There is no cause for plant snobbery here—no other group offers a greater variety of flower shapes and colors in plants that can grow close to provide endless enjoyment for months.

Small-space challenges

REGARDLESS OF THE OVERALL SIZE of the garden, there are small spaces to challenge your sense of proportion and use of color. Garden rooms are staples of landscape design and are especially effective for creating intimacy in large properties. They can be quite practical, too, like outdoor kitchens with herbs and vegetables in planters to mark their "walls." Some garden rooms cannot be considered small spaces, but others can be and there are twenty-first century trends that use the same ideas. Both rely on focal point, color harmony, and the succinct use of hardscape and plant materials to suit your site's scale and style. More and more, however, every inch counts for color in today's often smaller properties.

Entryways are universal, offer colorful opportunities to express yourself, and establish connections to the larger garden in mood and color. While every doorway is different, there are two major types of entries: public

---

Designing in a long, narrow space can mean vertical gardening and adding upright elements to extend the space's limits visually. This is an ideal location for this wondrous birdhouse collection and colorful container plants that pick up on their colors.

and private. Typically, but not always, the public entry is found at the front door while a private entry will open into a back or side door. The area around your front door can be a friendly, fast glance at your color palette. If you have a porch or stoop, this is the place to start, but even if the doorway is not sheltered, its colors should connect to yours.

In a patio home design, the entire postage stamp of a front yard can be considered the entryway. In each case, this small area will speak loudest with your dominant color and its color wheel opposite, such as purple with yellow or red with green. If you do not want the doorway to call out, use several shades of your signature color paired with cream or white. The front entry can be the lynchpin of symmetry between the garden and the house when you establish perspective using plants and color. If low shrubs line the path to the front door, consider a small flowering tree whose canopy reaches the eaves—cherry or apricot (*Prunus*) for spring, or summer's blue-purple chaste tree (*Vitex*). Eyes will follow the shrub line up the trees to the shelter of your front door. When the way is not clearly delineated, use the planting on each side of the door to its best perspective advantage. Symmetry is called for, but intentional mirror images can be disappointing. Equality in forms can come from diverse plants across your personal color spectrum; their scale can marry the entry to the garden beyond. Vary their heights with more intense colors framing the door or let their heights and colors step down. In this scenario, you repeat the door color at the opposite end of the space and let its shades lead your eye from that color to its mate, the front door.

Rear entrances are often the kitchen door with sidewalks and garage walls that need plants to soften their harsh lines. Consider the available space and sunlight here; paint and ornament may be the only options. Establishing shades of your dominant color here can mean careful choices but not much labor to install or maintain. There may be another exit, such as French doors onto a patio or deck, that demands a seamless transition to the back garden. This can be a seductive place: an arbor over the door covered in an evergreen vine, a huge rose (*Rosa*) trellis beside it, columns of Clematis, or a sequence of fragrant plants. This limited space need not be crowded physically when color makes the transition easily in either direction.

Design success in a small space depends on good use of scale to foster harmony and a mood of pleasant good cheer. In this case, the stones, ornament, and consistent color palette of green-, white-, and yellow-leaved plants provide a careful blend of sizes, shapes, and textures in sync with this peaceful water feature.

More popular than ever now is the idea to make the most of pocket rooms, small spaces created by the intersection of structures and plants. At least one side is a wall or tall hardscape such as you find in between houses on zero lot line properties. Of course, these walls and others, like the common wall of your patio and house, constitute a small space with tremendous vertical gardening potential. Be certain of its load-bearing ability, and your style to set up staging. Glass or painted shelves, rustic wood planters, stainless steel racks, or a row of pocket pots with a flat side—any of these can put garden colors into a small space with texture that suits your style.

Left: By placing pavers with planting space in mind, a quirky combination of plants with individual appeal becomes possible in a stylish setting. The intentionality of the design sets a round barrel cactus near colorful leafy edibles to charming effect in a small space.

Above: The addition of a water feature to small-space gardens expands their impact and your comfort zone right away. The gentle sound of flowing water, the play of light on the stones below, and ample and colorful plants ensure the chairs will be well used in this welcoming space.

Many gardeners harbor the desire for a surprise destination, a hidden view to be discovered with joy in every season. Such spaces have to be sought out on a footpath, maybe behind the hedge or under a draping tree canopy. You might adapt a color vignette from elsewhere in the garden in dwarf versions; a miniature Japanese maple (*Acer*) can echo the standard-size tree, for instance. If the hidden garden sits beneath a sweet gum tree (*Liriodendron*), its colors can mimic the red, purple, and gold shades of autumn, extending their seasons in the garden. For a bigger surprise, consider a small water feature surrounded by rich green ferns (*Athyrium*, *Polystichum*) and the white-wall effect of striped hostas.

Another colorful solution in small spaces that need help quickly: you can pop color in for a week with annual flowers or put colorful containers to work in four seasons if they are planted with dwarf shrubs and/or small trees. In season, pots of bulbs or tropical plants can bring exciting contrast, offer textures seen (or not seen, but needed) in nearby plantings, and deliver your colors throughout the garden.

Every idea that solves a problem depends on your execution to become reality. In the same way, each design relies on the plants you install to carry it out. You'll find plenty of options in the next chapter.

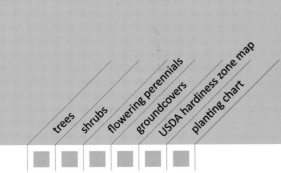

trees   shrubs   flowering perennials   groundcovers   USDA hardiness zone map   planting chart

Plants for nonstop color

PEOPLE TAKE DIFFERENT ROUTES to acquire plants, especially when it comes to the colors they choose. Some fall in love with plants on sight and put them wherever seems best to suit their latest idea. Others decide exactly what they want and search far and wide until they get it. Most of us, though, fall somewhere in between these extremes and have at least something of a plan in mind. We muse over possibilities that might accomplish our personal color goals and leave room for a few surprises. The plants in this chapter are organized to facilitate this process.

Four categories of plants are included here to represent the wide range of species, cultivars, and hybrids available. Trees, shrubs, perennials, and groundcovers are divided into groups by color: reds and pinks; blues and purples; yellows, oranges, and golds; greens; whites and creams; and neutrals, including grays and browns. The plant listings include botanical names for clarity, and the index lists them both ways. Common names are in regular type, genera and species are in italics, and cultivars are indicated with single quotation marks. The USDA hardiness zones are noted at the end of each entry. Numbers in parentheses indicate that the plant is considered marginally hardy in that zone.

So—have fun choosing your plants for nonstop color from top to bottom!

A visually effective front landscape design reflects its gardener's attitude toward the neighborhood. This great use of color sets a mood of attention to detail and warm welcome. The use of bold yellow black-eyed Susans call attention to the entrance with panache.

Trees

Ohio buckeye

Red buckeye

Buckeye

(Aesculus spp.)

There is a place for the woodsy charm of a buckeye tree in every garden and a species for every zone and locality. No other small tree has such huge, colorful impact and fabled history from coast to coast. The wood has long been beloved and put to important use for its carveable strength; buckeye has been fashioned into everything from baby cradles to artificial limbs. The trees vary in shape but are essentially pyramidal with distinctly hand-shaped, palmate leaves. Spring brings new growth that is light green with yellow and even pink hues. As they unfold, deeper green shades take over and are soon topped by red or yellow flowers that look like fat candles made to light up the shade. Buckeye trees are the stuff of children's imaginations, from red, yellow, or cream flower spikes to the nuts that split their shucks. They fall to the ground as the trees are revving their engines for fall, changing green leaves to fiery reds. The nuts are brown, from russet to mahogany, each with a lighter spot just made for your thumb. For centuries, they have been the American equivalent of a "worry stone," a talisman carried to absorb stress and bring good luck.

Six native species should be celebrated from north and east to south and west:

- **Ohio buckeye** (*A. glabra*) can be 40 feet tall in the wild but about half that in the garden. Its flowers are creamy yellow with red splashes, and the buckeyes sport spiny husks. Zones 4–7.
- **Painted buckeye** (*A. sylvatica*) has robust fists of flowers in clusters that live up to its name. The 20-foot tree has especially big leaves, and its blooms range from rose and pink to golden yellow. Zones 5–8.
- **Yellow buckeye** (*A. octandra*) dwarfs the others at 60 to 80 feet tall in the wild with blooms that demand a second look for their creamy yellow color with rosy red inside. Zones 4–8.
- **Red buckeye** (*A. pavia*) grows farthest south, a small tree (8 to 12 feet) that lights up the understory garden with coral-red pyramids of flowers. Zones 6–9.
- **Texas buckeye** (*A. arguta*) brings light yellow flowers in loose candle shape clusters to 20-foot trees, sometimes with a dozen leaflets on each hand. Zones 5–8.
- **California buckeye** (*A. californica*) dazzles with neat, creamy white flowers in a cylinder-shape rather like an old-fashioned baby bottle. Zones 6–8.

Birch trunks can stand alone and still draw a crowd. But crowded by brightly colored tulips, they assume grander status, like candles on a fancy birthday cake for weeks in spring. The contrast is stunning.

Magnolia grandiflora

Magnolia soulangeana

Magnolia

(*Magnolia soulangeana* and cultivars)

When someone mentions a magnolia, most people picture the evergreen tree with big, waxy white flowers synonymous with the Deep South. But the most colorful species, cultivars, and hybrids in this family are the deciduous trees that bloom before, with, or shortly after the leaves appear in spring. Most have slick gray bark and a spreading canopy or are grown with multiple stems that increase the number of flowering branches in these trees' jaw-dropping displays. Many are fragrant. The trees are usually 20 to 30 feet tall with a spread half as wide, but some are smaller. Leaf cover will be denser and flowers more plentiful in full sun. The blooms and buds can be pink, yellow, lilac, purple, or red, sometimes on the same flower as when darker buds open to reveal lighter shades inside. When fully open, some are perfect bowls while others have tall centers; most fall somewhere in between in their distinctive shape. Each flower is built of whorls, groups of petals stacked around their center.

The most venerable flowering magnolias are the **saucers** (M. × *soulangeana*), which are also known as tulip trees and Japanese magnolias. They can grow nationwide but some in this group are better suited to areas prone to late freezes than others. 'Alexandrina' sets the standard for classic rose-purple color outside and white inner petals. 'Burgundy' can match that

wine's color with especially shiny buds that glow in sunlight. Deep lavender with red hues in its outer layers, 'Picture' opens to expose a blush lilac interior framed by the darker tepals. Hybrids, cultivars, and selections from the flowering magnolias make for a complicated family tree. Pure white 'Pristine' honors its name with a simple white flower on a larger tree well suited to all zones, as are members of the Little Girl series, 'Jane' and 'Ann'. Bold red buds contrast with bright white centers on 'Jane', which is also noted for great fragrance and long-lasting blooms on a 15-foot tree. 'Ann' blooms early with pinky purple flowers and a spicy aroma. With great cold tolerance, 'Rose Marie' reliably blooms deep rosy pink. In warm winter areas, 'Heaven Scent' brings dark pink outer and purple inner petals. Yellow shades are well represented in 'Gold Crown' with warm tones in late flowers, while 'Elizabeth' offers brighter, daffodil yellow flowers. Oddly enchanting, 'Sunsation' buds are striped and open into yellow petals with dramatic purple centers.

Japanese maple

Red maple

Maple

(*Acer* spp.)

North America is known for its *Acer* species, both native and not. We grow a wide range, from towering sugar maples essential for syrup lovers to diminutive thread-leaf Japanese maples at the edge of a water garden. Various family members offer red flowers and new growth, dramatic barks, fine focal points, interesting textures, and fascinating fruits called samaras. Maple trees have evolved a most elegant means to ensure their future. The flying samaras are often a child's introduction to the species, and when Mother Nature's little helicopters spin off the tree, even adults can be forgiven for squeals of delight. The papery winged fruits carry precious cargo, often only one seed, and float as easily downstream as on the breeze.

Silver maple (*A. saccharinum*) is an eastern US native that matures at 50 feet or taller and provides multiseason color. Its green leaves backed with silver stir easily to animate spring and summer; fall colors may be red, orange, or yellow depending on the tree and cultivar.

- 'Silver Cloud', red-orange fall color, upright form, extreme cold tolerance
- *A.* × *freemanii* 'Autumn Blaze', an improved silver maple with bright red fall color in Zones 4 through 8

Broadleaf maple (*A. macrophyllum*) is native to the West Coast with leaves a foot wide or larger as it matures to 30 feet or taller. When the huge leaves turn yellow in fall, its gray bark with reddish ridges keeps the color going.

Red maple (*A. rubrum*) is a towering tree native to the eastern US with deep red flowers that appear before the red new growth, which soon turns green. Fall color is red or orange, as seen in 'October Glory' and 'Red Sunset'.

Paperbark maple (*A. griseum*) matures at 15 to 30 feet with fall color in different shades of green and red. Its cinnamon red bark soon peels away for increased interest all year. Some cultivars appear to be more cold hardy than the species, but their bark displays less contrast.

Japanese maple (*A. palmatum*) has deeply cut leaves and ranges from 4 to 25 feet tall. 'Sango-kaku', the coral bark maple, has bark that rivals its leaves for color. 'Bloodgood' (*A. palmatum atropurpureum*) delivers reliable deep red leaf color all season. Other notables include:

- 'Beni shichihenge' stuns with light green leaves and sweet pink edges.
- 'Shaina' has salmon-red leaves.
- 'Waterfall' is a small tree with fine textured, deeply cut green leaves, and a weeping form.

Quercus spp.

White oak

Oak

(*Quercus* spp.)

Every garden needs an oak tree for a colorful canopy from spring through fall and sometimes beyond. Oak leaves vary greatly in shape and size, but all can deliver slick spring greens, bold bottle greens in summer, and fall colors ranging from russet and orange to gold, yellow, and red. They offer soothing shade in a focal point tree that is equally stunning in winter. Where the trees are evergreen or semi-evergreen, their color holds the scene while most everything else takes a rest. Where they are deciduous, the bark and branches provide the garden design with beautiful stability and inspiring eye lines in grays and browns. The trees grow moderately fast while young and mature in sizes ranging from 40 to 80 plus feet tall and sometimes as wide. Oak trees reproduce by acorns that are prized by wildlife as much as growers. Their simple utilitarian purposes hide inside some of nature's cleverest handiwork. Acorns can be small as a shirt button or big as your thumb, round, oval, wide, or narrow, and some peek out of jaunty caps that seem made for elves. Each is a natural—and national—treasure delivered by native oak trees.

Three oaks represent the trees' best qualities and can grow in Zones 4 through 9:

- **Scarlet oak** (*Q. coccinea*) is true scarlet red in autumn.
- **Bur oak** (*Q. macrocarpa*) can grow 20 feet in 20 years and produces the biggest acorns.

- **White oak** (*Q. alba*) is a broad tree with shades of red fall color.

In more northern areas, Zones 4 through 7 (marginal at Zone 8a), three more oaks deliver big color and presence:

- **Chinkapin oak** (*Q. muehlenbergii*) brings orange and russet tones to autumn.
- **Northern red oak** (*Q. rubra*) delivers rich, dark red fall color.
- **Pin oak** (*Q. palustris*) has deeply lobed leaves that turn russet-bronzy-red.

Much of the country can enjoy these four oaks (in Zones 5 through 9):

- **Shumard oak** (*Q. shumardii*) has broad leaves and red-orange fall color.
- **Willow oak** (*Q. phellos*) has narrow leaves that turn brilliant yellow-orange hues and tolerates clay soils.
- **Sawtooth oak** (*Q. acutissima*) looks like it sounds with serrated leaves that glow golden yellow in fall.
- **Overcup oak** (*Q. lyrata*) offers wine-red bark and rusty yellow fall color in a lovely rounded tree that is drought tolerant.

Magnificent in warmer climes, **California white oak** (*Q. lobata*) shows fine drought tolerance and live oak (*Q. virginiana*) has classic spreading form. Both are essentially evergreen, pushing off old leaves with new ones.

Blackgum
(*Nyssa sylvatica*)

An old adage says that blackgum is never fooled, wait-ing to leaf out until all danger of a late spring freeze is past. It might as well be said that this tree is pre-scient about fall's arrival, too, since it begins coloring up several weeks sooner than most as if it knows what's coming. Yellow and orange hues appear quickly in late summer, then give way to purples and pure reds from scarlet to maroon in this tree, which is also known as black tupelo. Broad at the base and tapering to a point more than 30 feet above the ground, it redefines red fall color in native stands and modern landscapes. Lustrous and bottle green, blackgum's leaf shape is generally oval with prominent veins that give it a slightly coarse texture that allows sunlight to bounce around in every direc-tion. The flowers are yellow-green, arranged in pedun-cles, and give rise to small, thick-skinned blue drupes for added fall coloration on female trees. The bark is nearly black, ridged aggressively in channels that are even darker in hue and give a muted checkered effect at a distance. Cultivars gain more garden favor each year, including a weeping form, 'Autumn Cascades', and the especially colorful 'Miss Scarlet'.

Zones 4–9

Korean Stewartia
(*Stewartia koreana*)

A great small tree like this one lends quick visual per-spective to garden scenes created in flat, empty spaces. Stewartia takes on its mature form in a few years with sophisticated colors and habits that should be seen more often. At 20 feet tall and possessing a thick pyramid with showy trunks that peel dramatically, the tree can estab-lish scale in a focal point embellished with annual and perennial flowers as bigger, slower trees grow nearby. Bright white flowers stand out against arching, wine-bottle-green leaves in early summer. Opening like a single camellia, its velvety petals blush with a thick crown of buttery yellow stamens. Fall turns the leaves red unlike other autumn hues, more subtle and warm, closing in on orange at times. Equally beautiful flow-ers and even more prominent bark makes *Stewartia pseudocamellia* a good choice for larger spaces. Its check-erboard bark sloughs off in clever patching patterns; the tree tolerates moist soils, even clay. Its glossy dark green leaves turn deep reds in fall with overtones that range from muted oranges to dark purples. Silky stewartia (*S. malacodendron*) is native to the southeastern US. Its glorious fall color glows garnet red to deep purple even in warm winters.

Zones 5–8 (marginal at Zones 4 and 9)

Kwanzan Cherry
(*Prunus serrulata*)

Just as winter gives way to spring, troops of dancing flowers deliver Kwanzan cherry tree's surprising, strong pink-rose shades. Each bloom is doubled in form like tiny, eye-catching roses or camellias packed along the branches so tight it seems there's no room for leaves at all. The sight is a sure cure for the winter blues, and Kwanzan cherry continues to please as the flowers hold on while the pinky-bronze leaves emerge. Four- to 5-inch long, narrow, and slightly serrated leaves are also thick with a charming, slightly drooping habit; fall turns them several shades of red highlighted with bronze metallic tones. Beneath this colorful canopy, Kwanzan stands on attractive, striated bark in brown and gray hues that forms a rounded, vase-shaped tree. This tree sets the bar high for all other cherry trees but it is not alone in popularity. Sargent cherry (*P. sargentii*) is beloved for single rose-pink flowers, deep red bark, and bronze fall color in northern zones, while Higan cherry (*P. subhirtella*) offers a smaller, more open tree form well into the Deep South. The flowering cherry trees are uptown cousins of the native black cherry that do not fruit and so they are well suited for many garden styles and settings.

Zones 5–8

Smoketree
(*Cotinus* spp.)

You face a delightful dilemma when selecting a smoketree to light the garden in pinks and reds from summer through fall. Two species await consideration, one native to alkaline soils in the US (*C. obovatus*, also known as *C. americanus*) and the other from Europe (*C. coggygria*). Both may be seen as sprawling shrubs but deliver more drama in garden culture as small, colorful trees. The green-blue leaves let smoketree stand out among other trees in the early spring garden, but come May and June, it's all about the flowers. Spectacular, otherworldly, ethereal—these words are overused in most plant descriptions yet entirely apt for smoketree blooms. Up close, each flower is greenish yellow, exploding with countless pink hairs the color of cotton candy. Taken altogether they create color clouds that are frankly the prettiest "smoke" you'll ever see, floating above branches thick with oval leaves that turn striking red and purple plus yellow-orange in autumn. Adding to the choice dilemma, *C. coggygia* 'Royal Purple' lives up to its name grandly while the fall color on American smoketree is a brighter red. The native's bark holds great interest, a scaly brown canvas with a clever, flaking habit that gives it great dimension.

Zones 5–8

Strawberry Tree
(*Arbutus unedo*)

Evergreen trees that flower in the fall are a rarity in most places, including the zones where strawberry tree finds a home. The tiny white bells appear as balloons turned upside-down, ready to spill nectar out through each narrow neck. They hang in sweet clusters in a sharp contrast to the dark green leaves, but the blooms are not the most colorful feature of strawberry tree. That distinction is reserved for the red fruits that form round nubby orbs, each one no bigger than a pea. They gradually ripen to shades of red so brilliant it seems they would glow in the dark. A small tree no more than 15 feet tall, strawberry tree usually stands on one dark trunk that brings red tones to brown as it ages. Above is a dense canopy of perky, upturned leaves that are longer than they are wide. Native to warmer areas in Ireland and Europe, this species is one parent of *Arbutus × andrachnoides*, celebrated for rich hues in its burgundy-cinnamon bark. Cultivars of strawberry tree include 'Elfin King', which can bloom and fruit at 8 feet tall; 'Compacta', with charming, twisted branches for added interest; and 'Rubra', with pink flowers that open from dark red buds.

Zones 5–8

Chaste Tree
(*Vitex negundo*)

When the solid blue, nearly navy shades of chaste tree flowers greet you for the first time, you can be forgiven for wanting it in your garden immediately in its full-grown glory. Shaped like upside-down ice cream cones, the brilliant flower clusters explode upward from every stem in summer like organic fireworks made to celebrate Independence Day. They burst like a blooming halo above stacks of gray-green (or sage-colored) leaves that are slightly waffled, lighter underneath, and palmate with five fingers, rather like hands. Chaste tree is also called hemp tree to recall other leaves it resembles. The tree and its leaves have a pleasantly fresh fragrance, almost citrusy at times but never offensive, so it's perfect for planting where people can pass close by. This small and picturesque 15- to 20-foot tree is also listed in references as *Vitex agnus-castus* and is sometimes called agnus-castus too. In the garden, chaste tree has a sweet, almost quaint sprawling pyramid or arc shape that hums with bees all day during the long bloom season. Because the tree blooms on new wood, it can be pruned after blooming or when winter freezes its stems to maintain a pleasing height and shape.

Zones 5–9

Eastern Redbud
(*Cercis canadensis*)

Few trees are as likely to cause you to slow or even stop along your commute as eastern redbud on a spring morning. Its bare gray-brown branches burst with glorious, delicate blooms that crowd together along their length. Each tiny bead of a flower captures light like a prism and creates a blinding, radiant aura of the highest order—purple shades so rich with rose hues that their color needs a name of its own. But these are not just pretty flowers; they are a favorite nectar source for honeybees and butterflies such as Henry's elfin. They dazzle on a tree that can be 30 feet tall and about as wide in full sun, but in slightly shady woods will more often be seen 20 feet tall and more upright. Stunning, heart-shaped leaves open in olive green and soon develop brighter, deeper hues that add to the tree's considerable charms. Soon to follow are the seedpods, flat beans that speak of the tree's home in the legume family. Eastern redbud is widely distributed in a variety of environments and soil types; it is native to more than half the continental US and grows more widely.

Zones 4–9

Empress Tree
(*Paulownia tomentosa*)

There are trees that are much more popular with gardeners than with professionals in the field, and empress tree certainly is one. But all agree that the lavender-purple or purple-blue flowers are a powerful attraction to people and butterflies alike. The blossoms are even more spectacular because they appear before the leaves in a flowery cloud of hanging bells gathered into large panicle-shaped clusters that cover the tree. The shape of each flower resembles another spring favorite that shares its common name, foxglove tree, and in keeping with the royalty theme, some refer to it as princess tree. Whatever you call it, empress tree is an impressive tree even when not in bloom. The matte green leaves are lobed rather like those of catalpa and they are large, up to 10 inches across on a 40-foot tree. Densely arranged, the canopy of empress tree is a wide, shading beauty in summer with oblong yellow-green fruits that turn deep brown before they explode to send seeds flying. This habit can cause too many seedlings and give it the label "messy." No tree is for everyone, and empress tree is best grown in full sun where you can mow under it to control its prolific nature.

Zones 5–9

Harlequin Glorybower
(*Clerodendrum trichotomum*)

The late summer garden can benefit from cooling blue and purple tones, and harlequin glorybower delivers like no other small tree can. The tree's canopy is almost fluffy, full of dark green leaves that smell like peanut butter when crushed, giving rise to another common name, peanut butter tree. They make the perfect pillows to display huge clusters of pinky-lavender flower buds that pop open all summer to reveal fragrant white pinwheel flowers. There can be thousands of flowers on a 15-foot tree, and each one seems to attract butterflies in search of nectar. The white petals fall off to reveal incredibly beautiful bright blue fruit ringed by fuchsia calyxes that surround it like a star. The effect is dazzling—the blue is so shiny it looks like polished chrome. Most *Clerodendrum* species are tropical in nature, but this one performs best a little farther north, and if the top is damaged, it will resprout from established roots to bloom each year. 'Betty Stiles' is an especially nicely formed, cold-hardy tree that was originally found in North Carolina. Without much attention and planted in shade, harlequin glorybower becomes a huge thicket with fewer blooms and a propensity to spread unpleasantly.

Zones 6–9

Pawpaw
(*Asimina triloba*)

Unusual, colorful, and the source of delicious fruit, pawpaw tree should be celebrated in modern gardens. Native to moist, wooded areas such as creek banks in half the states, this small, unsung tree stands up to hurricanes as well as blizzards. Huge, sword-shaped leaves bring deep green tropical tones to this small tree, which can grow into a dense pyramid in sun or a looser form in shade. Both deliver color in their coarse texture but flowers and fruit are more abundant on sheltered, sunny sites. Pawpaws have been around since before honeybees, and so its pollinators are usually beetles and flies. The exotic flowers have evolved to attract the insects that prefer dark colors, intense odors, and easy access. They are deep purple-red, merlot wine shades and face downward as if to point their smell in the bugs' direction. It works and pollination happens to fruit-lovers' great delight. The light green, waxy fruits appear in clusters in the shade of the leaves, each 4 to 8 inches long and football shaped. Golden yellow with black seeds inside, the fruit tastes like banana custard. If you want fruit, seek out two different, commercially grown pawpaws; trees transplanted from the wild are seldom successful.

Zones 5–9

Purple-Leaf Plum
(*Prunus cerasifera*)

A tree bold enough to have "purple" in its name has to be great, and purple-leaf plum tree lives up to its billing. New leaves almost drip the color as they fill out, with deep shades that grow richer as spring hastens on to summer. Unlike other plants with purple new growth, this plum holds its color and enhances it in full sun and hot weather. Shade is a challenge, and leaves may be a puny green there. Moderately fast growing to about 25 feet at most, purple-leaf plum forms a rounded canopy that makes a fine specimen tree alone in the side yard or as the focal point in a mixed bed of perennials and bulbs. Flowers appear before the new leaves in very early spring. They are pink or white, thickly packed onto the tree with a smell much like an orchard of less lovely but edible plum trees in bloom. 'Purple Pony' has very dark rose-pink flowers, and both 'Thundercloud' and 'Newport' are noted for their dark leaf colors. Fruits do form on purple-leaf plum, little 1-inch jewels that can be purple, red, or even yellow depending on the cultivar chosen.

Zones 4–9

Rose of Sharon
(*Hibiscus syriacus*)

Althea, also called rose of Sharon, basks with cool blue style all summer in cottage gardens and offers stiffly upright vase-shapes to beds and borders in need of diverse silhouettes. Its flowers are open, single trumpets that resemble tropical hibiscus in that their petals seem to be made of slightly wrinkled paper, but they are unlike them in color. The dusky blues and purple that paint these blooms distinguish rose of Sharon from its family and are unforgettable in their simple perfection. Each has a bulls-eye center of deeper purple-red with a long pistil that pokes out boldly from the center like a nose laden with flower parts and pollen. The tree's interesting leaves are longer than they are wide and lobed rather like a chrysanthemum. Deep green and slightly shiny, they are loaded along each branch from top to bottom to create a perfect setting for the flowers on this small tree. Often seen in rows or planted in clumps, rose of Sharon can be pruned annually maintain it at the height (10 to 20 feet) best suited for your garden. Some trees are greatly improved upon by breeders, and there are fancier, often double-flowered, rose of Sharon trees that are lavender and rosy blue. But the classic cannot be beat for pure purple flowers and old-fashioned charm.

Zones 5–8

Sweetgum
(Liquidambar styraciflua)

Fall color can be amazing to view but bittersweet as it signals the end of a season. When leaves hang on longer than most other trees in exquisite purple shades, it is heartwarming to see and feel. Sweetgum is such a tree, with deep purple color dancing amid bold gold and red palmate leaf shapes on every branch. When at last they drop from the tree, its gray or brown bark is revealed with dark ridges that are often spaced neatly like lines on a graph. Its patterns are drawn on a sturdy trunk and spreading branches and make sweetgum tree easily recognizable against the winter sky. The new leaves emerge in spring with five or seven hand-shaped lobes. They are rich bottle green with petioles that are light in weight and color, so the new leaves rustle in every spring breeze. The purple feature has been enhanced in cultivars including 'Burgundy' and 'Rotundiloba'. The second of these is also fruitless, a desirable feature for those who consider the woody fruit called "gumballs" too messy for garden culture. Others love the fruit's spines and holes that resemble crazy organic space capsules; they may paint them in holiday colors or roll them in peanut butter and birdseed for outdoor decorating.

Zones 5–9

Chinese Pistache
(Pistacia chinensis)

This tree is a real showstopper all year because of its dynamic compound leaves—no one can resist taking a second look at close range or across the garden. Chinese pistache leaves are beautiful, highly sculptural, and gracefully gathered in a canopy shaped like a fancy parasol. The leaves emerge deep green in spring and hold their color through hot, humid, summer weather to turn brilliant autumn shades of orange, apricot, gold, and sometimes red. Most years, other orange leaf shades pale in comparison to this tree's colors, so intensely bright they almost look dyed. Every breeze puts them in motion for an unforgettable, kinetic garden moment. You might not notice long clusters of greenish flowers in spring, but you will when they become bluish red, deep blue, or bright red berries. They look like delicate jewels strewn among the orange fall leaves. But this tree is even tougher than it looks, with strong, durable wood that can stand up to high winds in exposed, sunny sites. A relatively fast grower to about 30 feet tall and almost as wide, Chinese pistache is nearly pest free and long-lived. Best in full sun and not picky about soils, it transplants readily and develops good drought tolerance.

Zones 6–9

Ginkgo
(Ginkgo biloba)

Renowned as the oldest living tree species on Earth, ginkgo (or maidenhair tree) uses color to charm in uncommon ways. Scalloped leaves emerge yellowish green and open into grass green, squatty triangles that give it another common name, duck foot tree. The tree can be more than 30 feet tall but is more often seen at that height; width varies but usually the tree presents an upright pyramid of bright, bold green. Like most trees, ginkgo needs regular water in its early years and becomes rather more drought tolerant as it ages; color will suffer without full sun and water in dry years. In transition to fall, when the leaves give up the green to reveal their trademark bright gold, the colors are briefly—and delightfully—striped in both shades on individual leaves. In fall, another natural surprise awaits when ginkgo leaves suddenly cascade off the tree as if a string was pulled to disconnect them. When the lawn suddenly wears a gold skirt at the base of the tree, its handsome gray trunks take the stage. Male trees are preferred, such as cultivar 'Autumn Gold' and the dwarf form 'Jade Butterfly'. The odor of female ginkgo flowers recalls rotting meat, and raking up the petals just spreads the smell.

Zones 4–9

Golden Chain Tree
(Laburnum × watereri)

Not to be confused with the Asian native golden raintree, golden chain tree is a long-beloved hybrid of trees from southern Europe. The small (20 feet) tree simply glows with spectacular color when in bloom, the quality that makes it a favorite focal point in cottage garden designs. Dangling chains of small golden flowers form fragrant clusters, called racemes, that are more than a foot long and taper perfectly into points below the leaves. The tree can display such dazzling gold and so many racemes in a row along a long branch that their silhouette may remind you of Chinese wisteria vines at their very best. Golden chain tree is a member of the legume family as evidenced in its pea-green, slightly pointed, tri-lobed leaves and long bean pods that form in summer. Young trees have green stems that change slowly to dark gray-brown marked with deep creases and crevices that grow more attractive with time. Golden chain's rewarding color can inspire love at first sight that forgives a few frailties, including the need to prune young trees into shape and the fact that all parts of the plant are poisonous. The cultivar 'Vossii' tolerates full sun without fading the fabulous flowers.

Zones 5–7

Golden Raintree
(*Koelreuteria paniculata*)

To see a golden raintree in bloom is to understand its common name. In late spring, every branch tip lights up with huge clusters of small golden yellow flowers that shower the tree in color. The tree's leafy canopy grows dense with so many little branches that there can be hundreds of these flower panicles on one 30-foot tree—the halo effect is simply brilliant. Native to Taiwan, golden raintree has dark brown, almost corklike ridged bark and surprisingly lightweight emerald green compound leaves. Each charming leaflet has gently scalloped edges and ruffles easily in the breeze. Golden raintree puts color in motion and keeps it there until late fall like few other trees can. Summer sees the flower clusters transform into wild arrangements of salmon-pink, papery envelopes, each designed to protect one precious seed. These dazzling structures are lighter than balsa wood but strong enough to carry the seed far and wide. And travel they do, becoming a pest in some areas of Zone 9. As they drop from the tree, the leaves turn yellow, and the gnarly trunks stand alone for a few months. Like few other trees, golden raintree starts conversations about the awesome quality of natural beauty, and deservedly so.

Zones 4–9

Pendant Silver Linden
(*Tilia petiolaris*)

More than one linden tree can do well in gardens across the center of the country, but pendant silver linden rises to the top of the family color chart. Big and little leaf lindens, Crimean linden, silver linden—all have jaunty, heart-shaped leaves on slick brown branches. Their trunks darken and crack nicely with maturity; the trees offer up pastel yellow flowers each spring, and most put on decent fall color. Pendant silver linden does it all better, displaying more and richer yellow blossoms in spring, matched by golden fall leaf colors. The tree is more oval and rounded than its relatives and creates a large, almost weeping form that could be taken for granted but for its strong colors. Fragrant little clusters of fringed yellow flowers extend from so many leafy branches that from a distance the tree looks like it is wearing a polka-dotted veil. When the leaves begin to turn, first fading then deepening to warm yellow-gold with red tones, they herald the season's change, and you know winter is approaching. The name of this tree is poetic, evoking images of fine handcrafted jewelry, and it does not disappoint.

Zones 5–7

Quaking Aspen
(*Populus tremuloides*)

There are a select few trees with uncompromising needs yet their astounding beauty beckons us to bring them closer when possible. As a group, poplar trees' finicky site needs and vulnerability to pests rate them low on the landscape satisfaction scale—the outstanding exception is quaking aspen tree. Forgive its flaws and use it where it can deliver unsurpassed color impact, most often in northern and western states where cool summers and relatively moist soils can support its pyramid of jewel-green leaves. With the first chill comes a huge color transformation; nothing else in the range offers anything close to these bright, richly yellow leaves. Each leaf is attached to its branch by an unusual stem that has the strength of a spider's web and is almost as thin. These petioles hold the leaves tight but any little breeze spins them into frenetic motion and causes them to shudder, to spin about like yellow tops in the air, to "quake." Just when you think the show is over, leaves drop to reveal the naked truth—quaking aspen's white trunk and angled branchwork is stunning against the winter sky. If you do not live where this tree can thrive, consider a pilgrimage to see it.

Zones 4–6

Sassafras
(*Sassafras albidum*)

Deep furrows mark the dark red-mahogany brown bark on sassafras tree and that might be enough to earn it a place in your garden. But there's much more to recommend this colorful native tree, starting with the way its narrow trunks are arranged and how its leaves are placed. Like a Hindu goddess's arms, the tree's side branches extend every which way, some go straight out and others bend sharply at the "wrist." Even without leaves their distinct geometry can be riveting. Glorious green, lobed leaves arise from each branch like extended hands with three stubby fingers that want to be seen. They splay out from the branches in tiers, revealing the wood behind. When the leafy layers color up in autumn, it is not possible to pass by a sassafras tree without a second or third look. Shades of orange, apricot, gold, and yellow paint each leaf like a patchwork quilt of perfect fall color, with a touch of navy blue sometimes added by fruits on female trees. Usually grown in the understory garden beneath taller trees, sassafras tree stands bright in the shade. The allure only grows when dappled sunlight illuminates it from above—resistance to its color is futile.

Zones 4–9

Tulip Poplar
(*Liriodendron tulipifera*)

You could look far and wide and never find a tree with flowers as colorful as the yellow and orange blossoms that crown tulip poplar each spring. But, its other colorful features distinguish it as well. Each flower actually does resemble a tulip in that they are open cup shapes, buttery yellow and bursting with orange inside. The flowers are followed by fruit capsules shaped like Christmas lights that are yellowish green and turn tan as they mature. A tulip poplar tree forms a single, thick gray trunk with slight ridges that are lighter in color at times in contrast to many native trees. Few side branches develop and the top growth is rounded in young trees but spreads with age. The leaves are recognizable from a distance, lobed with a deep notch on top in warm, green shades that are also hard to find. Tulip tree is host to larvae of the eastern tiger swallowtail butterfly; many others seek out its nectar as do hummingbirds, and a host of birds nest in the canopy. This is a large specimen, among the tallest native hardwoods, yet its habits and good looks make it a friendly, welcoming tree well suited for the modern landscape.

Zones 4–9

Bald Cypress
(*Taxodium distichum*)

If you think bald cypress only grows in the swamps of the Southeast, consider your horizons expanded because this graceful native tree enjoys a wide range of environments. This tree stands erect with a loose, flowing canopy that looks oddly light and soft for such a large tree; this effect is sometimes more pronounced in the West. Feathery, almost frilly, its new leaves are very light green in spring and deepen into jewel tones that soak up the summer sun and keep growing. The change of season brings out the best in bald cypress as green gives in to stunning golden-brown and rich russets to end the cycle. In colorful contrast, the gray trunk is coarse with sharp ridges and darker furrows in young trees. Over time the tree's base may split into lobes that form a big, scalloped, light gray skirt. Bald cypress trees are majestic when gray Spanish moss stripes their leafy branches. But the versatile tree is equally beautiful as the focal point behind deciduous shrubs or perennials in almost any garden soil. Such placement highlights its winter colors, which persist for weeks longer. One cultivar stands out for its bluish green color and narrower silhouette: 'Shawnee Brave'.

Zones 5–9

Dawn Redwood
(*Metasequoia glyptostroboides*)

Coast redwood (*Sequoia sempervirens*) and giant sequoia (*Sequioiadendron*) are ancient conifers long prized on the West Coast for their beauty and utility. Individual trees are impressive, huge, and dressed in thick clusters of deep green leaves that move with the wind; redwood groves are the stuff of poetry. Both these trees have limited habitat, and the 1941 discovery of dawn redwood, long thought to be extinct, added a dynamic upstart to this small family of magnificent trees. Dawn redwood has expanded the big tree's potential range to the East Coast and South, and its fans are both in residential and commercial landscapes. Finely cut leaves shimmer when fresh; light green new growth lays over the deep forest color of maturity. The effect is stunning, especially when sunshine plays around the tree in spring. Its pyramid shape is a naturally uplifting icon in the garden all summer, and when the leaves flame up into their orange fall colors, the effect is awe-inspiring. No tree bark can match dawn redwood's mature form. Trunks start with a red bark that darkens, cracks, and peels in charming narrow strips. In time the trunk gains the character of age, buttressing its crevices into deep cracks streaked in shades of gray.

Zones 5–8

Desert Willow
(*Chilopsis linearis*)

This little tree is a colorful garden elf—airy, finely textured, fern green leaves shaped like exclamation points, and clever hat-shaped flowers. Desert willow practically giggles as its loose canopy waves in the breeze. Each leaf may be a foot long but is never more than half an inch wide with a slightly drooping, kinetic nature. In all but the most humid environments, desert willow lightens the mood in borders and mixed hedgerows. But groups of the trees can be quite dramatic at the end of a sunny path in well-drained soil or a raised bed. The trumpet-shaped blooms appear on the current year's wood; thus pruning to shape does not hinder flowering. They are abundant in number and fragrance from spring through fall or longer in pastel pinks and violets, occasionally white, and sometimes red. They deserve your attention. Desert willow makes a fine large container plant where it is not hardy. Intergeneric hybrids are rare in nature, but desert willow is one parent of a delightful one, × *Chitalpa tashkentensis*. Its other parent is *Catalpa bignonioides*, and together they create a larger tree with bigger, pink-streaked blossoms. Like desert willow, this plant best suits dry climates.

Zones 7–9

Eastern Red Cedar
(*Juniperus virginiana*)

On the road to anywhere in the Midwest on a snowy winter day, eastern red cedar offers a crisp green salute to raise your spirits. Stiffly upright, this tree radiates green every day, all year, yet does not stay the same. Bright, rich summer color softens with the coming winter into darker greens with yellow and brown overtones. Male trees spew out yellow pollen clouds; females put on ice lapis blue cones, a much preferable quality. Unparalleled rot resistance and moth-repelling qualities have led to a host of uses for this tree. Historically, fence posts, storage closets, pencils, and hope chests are made of its wood, and more than a few of the trees have worn Christmas ornaments. Like many great native trees, eastern red cedar has given rise to cultivars better suited to landscape designs including the deep green, open form of 'Canaertii', long popular in the Midwest. 'Burkii' is prized for its open pyramid form; it develops oddly beautiful, purple tones in its winter leaves. Rich dark green leaves, long yellow cones, and shaggy gray-brown bark make an irresistible statement in incense cedar. The western native conifer, *Calocedrus decurrens*, has a similar pyramid form that ages into an upright column.

Zones 4–9

Japanese Privet
(*Ligustrum japonicum*)

When you seek a garden bed centerpiece or a colorful signature plant to repeat throughout the landscape, Japanese privet fits. It has been long appreciated as a hedge plant but is too often chopped into a shadow of itself to control its vigor. This 12- to 15-foot woody plant's best use is as a tree that delivers like the post office—consistently and year-round. The evergreen leaves are 2 to 4 inches long along lumpy (but lovely) light gray stems. Their color matches shiny dark green porch paint, and their heft lends a formal air to the dense canopy. Bright pyramid shapes made of flower buds appear at the branch tips in spring and soon open into scores of hairy little stars. The effect is like green glass bowls stacked with scoops of old-fashioned vanilla ice cream. Their fragrance is powerfully sweet, some say cloying, but you forgive that because it brings in the pollinating insects just when the garden needs them. The flowers become purplish gray fruits (drupes) that turn even darker in winter to bring more bold contrast to the tree. The cultivar 'Recurvifolium' sets the standard with gently waved leaves, and 'Nobilis' continues it with faster growth and glossier green color.

Zones 7–9 (marginal at Zone 6)

Lacebark Elm
(*Ulmus parvifolia*)

Trees that you choose for the front garden should be dramatically beautiful, long-lived, elegantly neat in habit, and easy to grow. Lacebark elm, also called Chinese elm, hits these essential points with dynamic color all year from coast to coast. First is its stunning rainbow bark that sloughs off with brown, orange, green, and gray hues, a quality that may explain its popularity as an urban street tree. Lacebark elm can be endlessly interesting to passersby even without its broad leafy canopy. Those leaves ride on a network of fine-textured branches that softens their deep green, leathery texture, gives the tree gentle motion, and creates excellent shade. Fall color tends to be yellow and rich wine reds, depending on location and the year. Lacebark elm has remarkable adaptability to a range of climate and soil conditions, and shows good tolerance for common pest problems. The trees can range in size from 30 to 60 feet and far outperform other non-native elms introduced in recent decades. The native elm, *Ulmus americana,* was lost to Dutch elm disease and has been the subject of many breeding efforts to replace its grandeur. The trees that result from those programs are worth watching with hopes for their long-term success.

Zones 4–9

Pines
(*Pinus*)

Garden design takes every sense into consideration, including sound, like the moans of high winds blowing through pine trees. Their visual appeal lies in their needles, bark, cones, and stately silhouette. Like puppies, pine trees vary greatly within the family and each has its charms. In Zones 4 through 7, Austrian and Japanese white pines (*P. nigra* and *P. parviflora,* respectively) are good examples of this diversity. The Austrian white pine can be 50 feet tall, eventually becoming a goblet shape of thick branches and dark green, almost-black needles. Its bark has dark ridges around stunning, abstract tiles in white and ashy gray. This is a dominant tree, meant to be seen from across the garden. Japanese white pine, though, covers itself in green-blue needles that sweep the ground, wide at the base and curving upward like a huge chocolate kiss. About 30 feet tall, this pine is at home in a range of garden sizes and styles. The American native white pine (*P. strobus*) has a broader range (Zones 4 through 8) and an elegant profile, like arms outstretched. In Zones 6 through 9, the resilient native American loblolly pine (*P. taeda*) has fine bright green needles, orange flowers, and tapered, 5-inch cones.

Zones 4–9

Weeping Willow
(*Salix babylonica*)

The lyrical songs and poems written about this tree are both ancient and modern. From the Koran and the Bible to Joan Armatrading and British duo Chad and Jeremy, weeping willows have evoked grand, often sorrowful emotions. The best known of its family, there is no better focal point tree for damp soils and those that are irrigated regularly. Numerous varieties with mature heights from 25 to 40 feet tall are favored in particular locales but the overall silhouette of this tree holds our hearts. In full sun, its weeping profile is distinct, branches that soar up and bend over just as far. They are thin and graceful, covered in skinny lance-shaped leaves that are 3 to 6 inches long and turn as yellow as a baby chicken in fall. Where there's space, grow a weeping willow for sheer drama. Other willows worth consideration for some zones include: white willow (*S. alba*), noted for huge size and diamond willow wood pattern brought on by a harmless fungus; purple osier or basket willow (*S. purpurea*), with colorful stems on a small tree; dappled willow (*S. integra*), for delightful variegated leaves and red winter stems; and pussywillow (*S. discolor*), the American native beloved for its fluffy gray catkins.

Zones 4–9a

Blackhaw
(*Viburnum prunifolium*)

Too few truly small trees make as big a color statement as blackhaw. No larger than 20 feet and often multitrunked, the tree is easily pruned to a rounded or more spreading canopy right at eye level. Leaves, flowers, and fruit are multicolored in multiple seasons. The 2- to 4-inch leaves are glossy green, rounded, and packed thickly onto gray stems that darken with age. In late spring, spectacular flower clusters decorate the tree like dollops of vanilla ice cream, scores of tiny white blossoms dropped on each branch. Part of blackhaw's charm is that the individual flowers sport skinny white filaments and yellow anthers so each cluster looks a bit unkempt, like a blonde with bedhead. The fruits, botanically known as drupes, have precious pink shades that slowly deepen as the summer wanes. Meanwhile, the leaves develop bronzy tones in summer that stand out in an understory garden beneath taller trees. The russet colors fade into a dull deep red in late summer but their display is not over—blackhaw leaves turn shiny red in autumn. The showy crimson tones are matched by beautiful clusters of oval-shaped, deep purplish blue drupes that hang on until late in the season, unless devoured sooner by hungry birds.

Zones 4–9

Castor-Aralia
(*Kalopanax pictus*)

Summer-flowering trees celebrate the season with panache, pouring out cool, colorful flowers as easily as you pour lemonade over ice on a hot afternoon. The creamy bloom clusters of castor-aralia bring an ethereal, light-hearted look to the garden when lawns and brightly colored flowers usually dominate. The end of each branch erupts with a wild display of round flowers, each one of dozens in the panicle held apart like starry balls on the toothpicks of their petioles. The light hues of the flowers range from nearly white to almost green; taken altogether, they seem to blanket the tree in mystery for weeks. When the same tree also offers eye-catching, shiny dark green leaves and rugged bark complete with thorns, it earns a place in the garden. This macho tree has deeply lobed, coarse-textured leaves cut like fat fingers to add an almost tropical flair to its garden presence everywhere it is grown. Native to north Asia, including Russia, castor-aralia grows more appealing each year as its upright form spreads to take on a rounded canopy. Its bark is fascinatingly dangerous: dotted with small, sharp thorns, it ages darker with intriguing, gray ridges in the mature tree that are mesmerizing all year long.

Zones 4–7

Catalpa
(*Catalpa* spp.)

Few trees bring delight when voracious caterpillars strip their leaves, but catalpas are the exception. Fishermen prize these caterpillars for bait; they collect and even freeze them for future use. The defoliation is natural and new leaves appear again soon after sphinx moth larvae (or "catawba worms") go into cocoons. Both Northern and Southern catalpas present unusual, colorful features besides their bright green, heart-shaped, matte leaves, each in its own distinct way. Northern catalpa (*C. speciosa*) and Southern catalpa (*C. bignonioides*) put on large clusters of white, ruffled trumpets. Bright white on a hot summer day, the clean, crisp, fragrant clusters are looser and larger in the southern tree. That makes it easier to see the bright yellow and sometimes purple markings in the trumpet's throat. The northern tree holds its blooms more upright and its limbs more erect than the southern, but both can reach 50 feet with little more than basic maintenance once established. The flowers soon become long, light green seedpods that give rise to the common name, Indian bean. They are dramatic, thick clusters of fine-textured beans that dangle below the coarse, darker leaves to light up the summer with colorful contrast.

Zones 4–9

Flowering Crabapple
(*Malus* spp.)

With numerous species and hundreds of cultivars, there is a flowering crabapple tree for every garden north of Atlanta, Georgia. They are medium-sized trees, each essentially a vase shape packed with flowers that appear before their leaves, abundant fruits, and reliable fall color. Pink or red buds open to pink and pinkish white flowers, creating a sweet cloud of color above thick, rich brown trunks in the early spring garden. The leaf canopy is medium green and dense all summer as the fruits, which hang like yellow and red earrings into fall, form when the leaves color up in shades to match. Modern cultivars also offer superior disease resistance and distinctive features. 'Liset' brings drama with deep red buds that open into rose-red flowers followed by bold maroon fruits the size of marbles. Pink buds and clear white, quarter-sized flowers make 'White Angel' a favorite in formal garden designs where its colors contrast well with brick and concrete statuary. 'Harvest Gold' is unusual and stunning. Pink flower buds open into white flowers, and little gold "apples" decorate it well into fall. Smaller than most, 'Narragansett' matures at 12 feet tall with red flower buds, white blooms tinged with pink, and cherry red fruits.

Zones 4–8

Flowering Dogwood
(*Cornus florida*)

Not many trees are capable of breathtaking flower display and long-lasting fall color in leaves and fruits. Sometimes reaching 30 feet tall, flowering dogwood brings these colorful features and an open form with limbs widely spaced when grown in part shade. In spring, the branches become arms dotted with pristine white blooms, each with four petals perfectly shaped around a simple center. In sunny sites, both branches and flowers will be packed tightly so bloom time becomes a blazing white blur that can stop traffic, in part because the sight is relatively rare. Shiny red, slightly elongated berries sit proudly all summer where the flowers were, usually in groups of five or more, waiting for wildlife to eat and disperse them. Even after they're gone, white stem tips remain as the leaves take on ruby red fall color. Dogwood is a native tree but suffers in prolonged drought. Farther north, another dogwood deserves attention: Kousa dogwood (*C. kousa*) covers each branch with white flowers in late spring followed by large red seed balls. The Asian native tree delivers brilliant fall color in purplish red and pure red. Its flowers are more pointed and closer together, stacked like whipped cream and almost obscuring the leaves.

Zones 5–9

Star Magnolia
(*Magnolia stellata*)

A small tree, usually no more than 20 feet tall, upright, and about 15 feet wide at most, star magnolia more than lives up to its name. The spectacular and fragrant starry flowers appear in late winter or early spring, covering the tree's round canopy with pristine white pops of color. Rows of narrow, slightly curled petals are stacked around a neat cream center; they are light enough to flutter in a slight breeze. Star magnolia brings a hopeful mood to stir the season's optimism, and the tree is beautiful alone or in a row at the back of a long border. Lancelike leaves follow the flowers; they are crisp green all summer, then slightly yellow-umber in fall. Green pods form in summer and then split open to reveal shiny scarlet seeds in late autumn. The tree can fill both color and culture needs in the garden. It is a bright light to curse winter away, thrives in moist areas, and can bloom in shade at the edge of a wooded area. The cultivar 'Centennial' is taller and more vigorous and pyramid-shaped than the species. 'Royal Star' blooms slightly later and so better escapes late freezes to flower when the species does not.

Zones 4–8

Sycamore
(*Platanus* spp.)

Across the country, many new homesites are a blank slate. They need color in a big way, and the right big tree to set the scene. American sycamore (*P. occidentalis*) puts color into every design element, from its stately form covered in huge green leaves, to textural contrast in rounded fruit that is lighter green all summer. Fall turns the leaves brown and tan and after leaf drop, the sight of its creamy bark with rough brown peels provides a winter muse for artists of all sorts. Sycamore reaches 70 feet or taller and spreads nearly as wide, with native habitats along streams and rivers from Canada to Texas and east. It is equally at home in garden soil with irrigation in dry seasons. As tall but not as wide, London planetree (*Platanus* × *acerifolia*) graces cities worldwide because it tolerates urban environments and common diseases better than sycamore. As a young tree, it has darker leaves and a more upright shape but matures with the same spreading form. Planetree bark has a more spotted pattern in shades of reddish brown and cream that is equally impressive in winter. Both *Platanus* trees provide imposing, colorful charm and can be the only tree your garden needs.

Zones 4–9

American Hophornbeam

(*Ostrya virginiana*)

Whether tree bark peels to relieve a tree of pests or just to show off in winter, gardeners revel in the natural, if disconcerting, process. American hophornbeam puts brown shades front and center in winter but a closer examination reveals this tree's particularly attractive patterns. Narrow strips curl up, still firmly attached and oddly fringed, like Easy Rider's iconic western jacket. Milk chocolate brown, tan, and gray mark the trunk in eye-catching linear patterns that invite a closer look even when the tree has leaves but are most dramatic without them. Hophornbeams are 20 to 40 feet tall and almost as wide when they're mature; they form a rounded pyramid shape that shows off forest green, serrated leaves that can be 5 inches long tapering to sharp points. They are the perfect backdrop for light green fruits in little cocoon shapes that adorn the tree in summer like finely crafted earrings. Fall color is briefly yellow-brown and soon gives way to the amazing bark display. American hophornbeam's appeal extends to its ability to tolerate alkaline soils well and hold its own as a full sun street tree as well as in the understory beneath other stately trees. It is underappreciated yet once you see it in winter, you will never forget the statement it makes then and all year.

Zones 4–9

Crape Myrtle

(*Lagerstroemia* hybrids)

When the parents of a crape myrtle include the hardy *L. faurei*, they are reliably hardy far north of their previous southern range. Besides selecting for cold tolerance and flower colors, modern crape myrtles were bred for their spectacular barks that grow more attractive as the trees age. White, creams, and an array of grays, plus every shade of brown in the crayon box from cinnamon to rust and mahogany, these barks peel grandly. The trees perform well in almost any well-drained soil and full sun, and mature to heights from 20 to 30 feet or more. Their flowers range widely from white to pinks, purple, and red.

'Lipan' is a small crape myrtle (20 feet) whose white bark peels away to reveal dark, cocoa-brown beneath. 'Tuscarora' is also small, with cocoa patches under sandalwood brown bark on a neat, vase-shaped tree. 'Biloxi' stands taller; it has coffee-bean-brown bark with greenish gray and tan underneath.

'Miami' has light gray bark that exfoliates to show off patches of red-brown and bone colors that can be quite mottled. 'Wichita' displays bark that is russet-potato brown and red mahogany on tall, upright trunks. 'Natchez' is tall with the reddest cinnamon shades revealed under tan and cream bark.

Zones 6–9

Downy Serviceberry
(*Amelanchier arborea*)

Designing a "naturalized" area in a modern landscape can be challenging, but this native American tree can establish that "wild" mood nearly by itself. Even if downy serviceberry had no other qualities to recommend it, its dynamic form and sleek gray trunks certainly would. The bark is beautiful in winter, streaked in shades that range from storm cloud gray to charcoal on gently curved trunks and thick branches. Depending on the site, downy serviceberry ranges in height from 20 to 40 feet tall with trunks that can be thick as an elephant's leg and widen to a fat "foot" or base. Attractive all year, its features include fuzzy white flower and crisp dark green leaves that exhibit autumn shades from apricot to orange and reds. Striking blueberry-like fruits complete the package, prized by birds and humans alike.

One natural hybrid of the group has the deservedly boastful name *A. × grandiflora*, or apple serviceberry. This tree averages 20 feet and as wide if left to form a thicket, maintaining the rich gray trunk and branches of its parent. It is further distinguished by purple new growth. Apple serviceberry cultivars feature strong red fall color and include 'Princess Diana', 'Autumn Brilliance', and 'Ballerina'.

Zones 4–9

Japanese Zelkova
(*Zelkova serrata*)

Not every tree has attractive yet different bark in youth and old age. When it also makes a striking shade tree and maintains good looks all year, it becomes a winner for modern garden designs. Japanese zelkova debuts with dark trunks and branches that are glossy, like the shiny red colors of cherry wood. Mature zelkovas display storm cloud gray bark that flecks off to show red-orange tones in pockets all over the trunks. Native to Japan but also Korea where it is much beloved for its tenacity, zelkova is said to invoke a mood of tolerance and goodwill. Its name, however, comes from two words in the native language of the Republic of Georgia that mean "bar" and "hard," a reference to the durable wood. Growing slowly to grand heights (60 feet or more at times) this tree establishes an erect posture. Its canopy is a fountain of leathery leaves that spread to shade a street, a walkway, or a bench in the backyard. Fall color offers gold and purple as the leaves prepare to drop off a sturdy tree that has the good looks of an elm but resists its pests and also tolerates heat and humidity.

Zones 5–8

Paperbark Maple
(*Acer griseum*)

No other maple has trunks and branches as beautiful as the paperbark does. This tree gains new fans each time it is seen in the winter landscape where its colors bring vibrant contrast to gray skies and snow banks. The bark peels in muscular fashion as if it would rip off the tree painfully, in clutched red fists. That does not happen yet the colors beg a second—and third—look. Paperbark shades encompass reds from sienna to rust, sepia, and cinnamon as the peels twist away to reveal gnarly levels below. When spring arrives, the canopy takes on its summer cover of greenish blue leaves that have three distinct leaflets forming a triangle called a trifoliate leaf. The trees thrive in full sun and almost any soil that drains. Not taller than 30 feet but thick with branches, paperbark maple puts a primal beauty in your face as a focal point tree to be seen and appreciated all year long. Another trifoliate (or trident) maple, three-flower maple (*A. triflorum*) brings especially attractive, if different, peeling bark in chocolate brown and ash gray to the scene. Both of these maples display red fall color, but it is more robust in the three-flower maple.

Zones 4–8

River Birch
(*Betula nigra*)

At every formal gala, there are many beauties but one always stands out; it is the same among trees. The tall "drink of water" in an Emerald City-green gown gets attention, and if she has nice legs, your glance lingers. So it is with river birch—that first glimpse can start a lasting love affair. In this case, it is the "legs," the tree trunks that are so enticing, especially because they are usually seen in multiples that further increase the attraction. But single trunked or in classic triples, river birch bark puts on a show all year with bark that peels, curls, and colors like few can do. Every shade from white through gray and cinnamon are grandly revealed in curiously charming, wide curls. Slipping out from under the leafy canopy of small, puckered leaves with toothy edges or revealed in all their winter glory, river birch bark is unforgettable long after that first glance. The trees can be as tall as 60 feet eventually, but begin their show much sooner, at about 10 feet, and only get grander year by year. They are covered in draping swaths of leaves that rustle in the breeze until autumn turns them yellow and casts them aside.

Zones 4–9

Shrubs

Winterberry

Blue holly

Holly

(*Ilex* spp. and cultivars)

There's more than meets the eye in hollies: shrubs large and small, with and without thorns, berried or not, solid green and variegated leaves, evergreen and deciduous. Each plays an important role in modern garden design with unstoppable color year-round. Some holly "bushes," as they are called, are often featured in foundation plantings because no matter the weather or conditions, they never flag. Thick with leaves, the shrubs keep the scene neat around the front door or in thorny, impenetrable hedges. But larger hollies make strong statement plants in a border where evergreen leaves or berry showers (on deciduous selections) become winter anchors for the design. Theirs are the brightest winter reds—at least until you clip them for holiday decorating or the birds make a buffet. These plants can be big berry makers, as long as both male and female plants are included. The dependable nature of hollies finds a home in every zone, depending on the variety selected.

Native American hollies are a varied bunch that show off the best facets of the group. Inkberry (*I. glabra*)

takes its name from its showy black fruits. The small leaves are glossy and bright green when they're new, and take on blue tones as they mature. Indestructible **yaupon holly** (*I. vomitoria*) almost belongs in a class by itself for strident good looks in an assortment of sizes and colors. Truly dwarf specimens, accent plants, and taller dense thickets may have red, orange, or yellow berries. Deciduous hollies have a special place in gardeners' hearts. Southern states have **possomhaw** (*I. decidua*), and everywhere, **winterberry** (*I. verticillata*) delights gardeners in late winter when its thickets explode with orange-red berries hiding in the leaves until they drop off. Slow-growing to about 10 feet tall, 'Cacapon' and 'Winter Red' are superior selections, and the smaller 'Red Sprite' brings its defiant beauty to any size garden.

When a wonderful plant originates outside the United States it is called "exotic," and we embrace them if they are well behaved and bring extra panache to the garden. **Blue holly** (*I. × meserveae*) is especially dramatic with a spooky blue cast to its spiny leaves in contrast to scarlet red berries in the Meserve series. 'Blue Girl' and 'China Girl' are excellent in Zones 4 through 7. **Japanese holly** (*I. crenata*) has small leaves with no spines in rich, forest evergreen colors. For fine texture on a small or medium-sized dense shrub and black berries, consider 'Convexa' and 'Glory' in Zones 5 through 7.

Roses decorate landscapes nationwide with good reason—no other shrub equals the passion they inspire in gardeners. Climber and shrub types play equal roles in this landscape for color and a dignified air of old garden style.

Japanese spirea

Spirea spp.

Spirea

(*Spiraea* spp. and cultivars)

Spireas first became popular as big shrubs with a blaze of white glory in their spring flowers, but now their beauty spans the seasons and the nation. More colors and sizes await to deliver texture in color to every garden style. Spirea leaves vary from the blue-green color of a tropical lagoon to screaming yellows, all striking and mostly fine-textured. The plants have scores of woody stems that form thickets ideal for resting wildlife. The shrubs have different flower arrangements that may appear in spring or summer, or both. Some are single, others are in clusters that may be round or flat, yet all have that intangible quality that attracts and holds your interest year after year.

There are two distinct kinds of spireas, bridal wreath and Bumald, separated by the arrangement and timing of their flowers. The basic spirea flower has five flared petals that are sometimes separate from one another but are most often cupped like a horn. **Baby's breath spirea** (*S. thunbergii*) is the earliest bridal wreath type to bloom and can be downright breathtaking in early spring. Its tiny white flowers have flared petals open like a fairy's peaked hat amid lime green leaves that are small, feathery, and soft to the touch. The classic bridal wreath is **Vanhoutte spirea** (*S. × vanhouttei*), which sets the bar for this group and sets it high. Vanhoutte covers an exuberant fountain shape with leaves that are dark green with a blue cast and buckets of flower clusters in orbs that look like little white nosegays. **Reeves spirea** (*S. cantoniensis*) has double flowers on a similar shrub.

The **Bumald spireas** (*S. × bumalda*) are hybrids of two Asian species and selections taken from them. 'Goldflame' started the trend toward these smaller spireas with graceful 3-foot mounds. In early spring, new leaves emerge in fiery red-orange shades that fade to yellow. Its sweet pink flower clusters are characteristic of the Bumalds, flat-topped and plentiful. 'Goldmound' has a richer, buttery yellow color that lasts all year and pink flowers that are small but bright. 'Lime Mound' begins the year with new leaves that are bright orange and turn a steady lime green; its flowers are slightly more purple than the others. 'Anthony Waterer' has become the name for several similar shrubs with reddish green leaves and rosy pink flower clusters. One of them is 'Crispa' noted for its incredibly fine, twisted leaves that are sometimes variegated. You will find brighter pink flowers in 'Froebelii' and 'Gumball'.

Sungold

Albury purple

St. John's Wort
(*Hypericum* spp. and cultivars)

Yellow-flowering shrubs are an uncommon treat anytime, and those that deliver summer color are even more precious, drawing in scores of bees. St. John's wort is a diverse group of shrubs with sunny yellow blooms that ranges from quaintly small to good-sized and garrulous. These worts (the traditional word for "plant") are native to temperate zones in the US and around the world, beloved for their complicated flowers, and respected for their herbal properties. The plants take their common name from St. John the Baptist, whose birthday is celebrated in June when the plants bloom. The flowers vary slightly in their warm yellow hues and attitude but all have five petals that open to reveal prim halos of yellow stamens; many form attractive fruits. The plants display bright green or green-blue leaves that have evolved to suit their wide range of native habitats; some are deciduous while others are semi- or completely evergreen. The *Hypericum* genus offers a size and shade for many designs that seek yellow in a sunny or partly shady garden. Despite their native origins, they are surprisingly underused and so make loud, colorful statements in every zone. An excellent St. John's wort for Zones 4 to 7 is **Kalm's SJW** (*H. kalmianum* 'Ames'), an evergreen with brilliant golden yellow flowers. Its upright branches cover a 3-foot mound of blue-green leaves that are longer than wide. Especially stunning, although limited

to Zones 5 through 7, **Albury purple** (*H. androsaemum*) puts on rich golden flowers with chart-topping clusters of 10 or 11 flowers in each. Its spectacular maroon berries often last for weeks after the purplish green leaves are gone.

In Zones 4 through 8:
- **Great SJW** (*H. pyramidatum*) features an upright growth habit (5 feet by 3 feet) and saffron yellow flowers with lush, glossy petals in large center clusters.
- **Sungold** (*H. patulum*) thrives in wet soils, a perky, rounded mound (3 feet by 3 feet) of flowers with very prominent bright yellow stamens.
- **Sunny Boulevard** (H. 'Deppe') features small, almost daffodil-looking flowers on a similar small shrub that blooms beginning in mid-summer; its narrow leaves are deciduous.

In Zones 5 through 9, 'Hidcote' SJW (*H.* × *Hidcote*) has a long bloom season on a slightly larger, 4-foot mounded plant. 'Sunburst' (*H. frondosum*) is larger still (5 feet by 5 feet) and is drought tolerant once established in Zones 6 through 9. Its spectacular flowers look like lime yellow lollipops. They soon burst open dramatically and cover the shrubs.

Koreanspice

Burkwood viburnum

Viburnum

(*Viburnum* spp. and cultivars)

Viburnums are garden soldiers, stalwart staples for year-round good looks and color that stand at attention through snow, thunderstorms, and summer heat. They never complain, seldom need much attention, and so are taken for granted and sometimes considered old hat. But tried-and-true colors, elegant forms, and great diversity mark this group and can make selecting just one quite a challenge. One may be a featured player in all its glory or a dozen can stand close to elevate a hedgerow. Viburnum leaves can be coarse-textured and waffled or smooth, shaped like fat footballs or maple leaves. Fall colors are sometimes golden but may also offer every deep red and purple shade imaginable. The often-fragrant flowers gather in clusters that may be larger than your fist and very dramatic or tiny and barely noticeable. They are usually white or cream, or rarely, sweet pink as if they were blushing from the sudden attention they get in spring. You cannot overlook the charming fruits, which often undergo mind-boggling color changes from summer into fall. The name "viburnum" comes from the Latin for "wayfaring tree," which might refer to the way they spread. Thanks to the birds that devour the fruits and then deposit the seeds far away from the mother plant, there is no shortage of *Viburnum* species. These can be huge, back-of-the-border shrubs or quite small in the case of dwarf varieties. The best, most colorful ones mature between 6 to 8 feet tall and wide.

- **American cranberrybush** (*V. trilobum* 'Bailey Compact'). Burgundy fall color and persistent red fruit, Zones 4–7
- **Nannyberry** (*V. lentago*). White "snowball" flowers, purple berries, yellow-orange fall leaf color, Zones 4–8
- **Mapleleaf viburnum** (*V. acerifolium*). Creamy white "snowballs," shiny purple berries, fall color gold to purple, Zones 4–8
- **Arrowwood** (*V. dentatum*). Not as showy with small flowers and brilliant blue berries in summer that turn black, prized by wildlife, yellow fall color, Zones 4–8
- **Doublefile** (*V plicatum* f. *tomentosum*). Tiered rows of big flat flower clusters, red fruits turn black fruit, Zones 4–8. Stellar selections include 'Pink Beauty', 'Mariesii', 'Shasta', and 'Summer Snowflake'.
- **'Mohawk' Burkwood viburnum** (*V. × burkwoodii*). Red buds open with white flowers, red berries, orange-red fall color; Zones 5–8.
- **Smooth witherod** (*V. nudum* 'Winterthur'). Small white flowers, bright pink fruit turns deep blue. Shiny, leathery leaves turn wine red and maroon shades; Zones 5–9.
- **Koreanspice** (*V. carlesii*). Pinkish flowers, vibrant red berries, and toothy deep green leaves, Zones 5–9

Burkwood Daphne

(*Daphne* × *burkwoodii*)

People either love or hate daphne shrubs. The latter camp insists they are finicky divas, as likely to croak as they are to reward with colorful arias. Ally yourself with the lovers and provide well-drained soil that is richly organic and provide plenty of water regularly in sun or shade. Burkwood daphne drapes its shapely, almost evergreen leaves in a cloak of purplish pink flower buds that are fat with expectation. They open into tight corsages of star-shaped blooms that are white tinged with pink and extremely fragrant. The flowers give way to scarlet red berries that last from summer to fall. For an even brighter spot in the garden, choose 'Carol Mackie' for its leaves edged in white. With both buds and flowers in rosy pink shades and neat habit, this daphne lights up a shady spot all year. Put up a "do not disturb" sign and let daphne find her voice in your garden. In two seasons this shrub's ebullient form will enchant you, and once it blooms, you will be hooked. Although daphnes can adapt to soils that are acid or neutral in pH, rose daphne (*D. cneorum*) offers strong rose pink flower colors in looser clusters and grows well in rocky soils.

Zones 4–8

Flowering Quince

(*Chaenomeles* 'Texas Scarlet')

Spring can start sweetly with a crocus or some other fairly subtle plant, or you can kickstart it with bright red 'Texas Scarlet' quince. The typical flowering quince has precious salmon flowers, blooms for about a week, and then disappears into a green blob of leaves. 'Texas Scarlet' represents the best of this shrub's modern incarnations: it is a showstopper at about 3 feet tall and up to 5 feet wide. Arching upward with exuberance, each branch shines with fat clusters of cardinal red flowers, each open just enough to see the yellow stamens in its throat. Glossy and round green leaves 1 to 2 inches long and wide grow thickly to make 'Texas Scarlet' a shapely shrub deserving focal point status in the spring garden. Adaptable to most soils but not drought tolerant, modern flowering quince shrubs need not be relegated to the backyard. These are real showoffs for red in spring, with strong shapes and handsome leaves to carry on for the rest of the year. A bit larger shrub with flowers the color of Dorothy's ruby slippers, 'Scarlet Storm' offers added drama. This and other lovely quinces in the Double Take series were introduced by North Carolina's Tom Ranney.

Zones 5–9 (marginal at Zone 4)

Japanese Barberry
(*Berberis thunbergii* f. *atropurpurea*)

Reds—deep scarlet, maroon, and almost purple—make the leaves of Japanese barberry a hallmark for garden color. Its optimistic form, red-brown thorny branches, and red berries make it a must-have when you seek texture contrasts in shrub plantings. But the variety in color and size of its leaves takes Japanese barberry to the next level of desirability because the group is so diverse. They range from little ones like 'Bagatelle', barely 2 feet tall with coppery red and green leaves, to the upright 'Helmond Pillar', covered in bold maroon, to the broad, almost perfect hedge form of the species itself. About an inch long and dotting the many complex, and interwoven branches, the leaves may be red, purple, or shades in-between. The brilliant ruby red berries appear in summer and can last six months unless, as often happens, they are devoured by hungry birds. The shrub is usually maintained at about 4 feet tall and wide, and grown in full sun where its colors will be at their best. Although it tolerates most soil conditions, this is not a plant for boggy sites. Its thorns make Japanese barberry an effective but beautiful barrier plant. Cultivars with variegated leaves include 'Rose Glow' with pink and purple leaf patterns.

Zones 4–8

Mountain Laurel
(*Kalmia latifolia*)

You may be surprised to learn that a shrub with the word "mountain" in it can grow almost anywhere, but that is the case with mountain laurel. This native American species is known for pink and white flowers as well as a large, rounded shape in sunny gardens and a slightly looser, some say more attractive, form in part shade. Its evergreen leaves are rich dark green and shiny with neatly pointed ends held out like open arms in a welcoming embrace. Each branch explodes with spring clusters of buds that are every bit as attractive as the flowers they hold inside. The species is lovely, but the variety 'Ostbo Red' mountain laurel is among the best of the selections and cultivars chosen for both its smaller size (5 to 7 feet tall and wide) and smashing crimson color flower buds. As if they know how gorgeous they are, the buds stand up on stiff stems for weeks before they finally begin to open. The flowers are blissfully slow to show their baby pink interior petals, so 'Ostbo Red' is covered with buds and petals at the same time in a truly memorable show. Like many native plants, mountain laurel grows well with few problems in well-drained soils.

Zones 4–9

Ninebark

(*Physocarpus* spp., cultivars, and hybrids)

Too few shrubs are known for their amazingly colorful bark but this American native outdoes them all.
Ninebark gets its name from its bark's peeling habit;
curls strip themselves off to reveal outrageous shades of
red and brown in the winter garden. The beautiful leaves
emerge, shovel-shapes with gentle lobes and distinct,
taut veins with outstanding texture. The flowers are pink
or whitish pink, grouped in oval-shaped, flat-headed
clusters that become shiny red fruits. At a size of 8 feet by
6 feet, ninebark creates an imposing presence in sunny
sites. Smaller selections are even more popular because
they add colorful leaves and more compact forms to the
plant's sometimes-rangy profile. Golden leaves that turn
lime green and surround the red fruits mark 'Dart's Gold'.
'Amber Jubilee' marks its leaves in rich gold and orange,
then turns them dark red and purple in fall. 'Coppertina'
looks like it sounds, bronze new growth with chartreuse
tones in their heart. By summer, the leaves are copper
red, deep in contrast to pale pink flowers and striking
against its red fruits. It is not as vase-shaped as 'Summer
Wine' can be. This one has redder leaves, almost purple,
pink flowers, and an exuberant vase silhouette like its
relatives, the old-timey spireas.

Zones 4–7 (marginal at Zone 8)

Piedmont Azalea

(*Rhododendron canescens*)

It's not necessary to live in the Piedmont to enjoy the
explosion of pink that is this azalea. All you need is a
desire to expand the early spring garden with a plant
that redefines the terms "shrub" and "pink." No amount
of pruning will make this plant a hedge, and its strongly
upright form means it works best as an understory
or border background choice. But even in deep shade
where its branches stretch awkwardly, this is not a
tree, so shrub it must be. Piedmont azalea, also called
Pinxter azalea or bush honeysuckle, glows with blush
pink buds with rosy tubes that open into shapes more
like a Japanese honeysuckle than most azalea flowers.
Pale, almost lavender lower petals reach out like launch
pads for the long, curvy pistil and stamens. These wispy
flower parts are featured in the species, and the cultivar
'Varnadoes Phlox Pink' has even deeper pink buds and
pinker flowers. Piedmont azalea thrives in sunny and
shady gardens, any acidic soil, and for most of the year
is a rather gawky green presence like a vase on stilts. The
flowers appear just before the leaves with a sweet but
strong fragrance reminiscent of cloves.

Zones 5–9

Red Osier Dogwood
(*Cornus sericea*)

A classic Christmas card depicts a snow bank with red osier dogwood stems popping out all over it, their brilliant red brighter than Santa's hat. They are stunning even without the snow, leafless and held straight up like pointed cherry-red arrows flashing warm messages in the coldest winter landscape. Few shrubs garner as much attention in one season and few deserve it. Especially in designs weighted heavily toward spring and summer color, a hedge or slope dotted with the upright vase form of red osier dogwood bridges the seasons with panache. Since new stems are more brightly colored, gardeners either prune out one-third of old ones each year or cut the entire shrub down every other year. Its colorful profile is not limited to winter, however, and includes delightful drupes that are white with a blue cast and fall color in red-purple hues. Red osier dogwood thrives in sunny or shady sites, in richly organic soils with plenty of water, even boggy conditions. Only slightly less vibrant, red twig dogwood (*Cornus alba*, especially the variegated 'Elegantissima') tends more toward the purple shades in its stems. Equally attractive but usually larger and thicker, its flowers are sometimes more fragrant.

Zones 4–7

Shrub Rose
(*Rosa*)

People are of two minds when it comes to shrub roses—they dismiss or embrace them, often for the same reasons. Compared to hybrid tea roses, shrub types are very easy to grow since they seldom, if ever, require pest control. Few shrubs bloom as often as a remontant (reblooming) rose, and with heights that range from less than 2 feet to nearly 5 feet, there's one for every sunny garden space. These qualities can seem understandably elementary to veteran cut-flower rosarians. However, the rest of us appreciate them as well as the neat rounded forms and flower colors in every shade of rose and pink. Flower sizes vary almost as much; let the last flush make scarlet red hips in fall. Use the shrub rose to establish your hue as a hedge or to put the color twist of repeated bloom flushes into a mixed shrub row with spireas and hydrangeas. This class of roses thrives in well-drained soil and once established needs no more water and fertilizer than other flowering shrubs. There are two different sorts of shrub roses: antique or old garden roses, and modern introductions such as the David Austin roses and KnockOut roses. Shop locally for suitable varieties.

Zones 3–9

Spreading Cotoneaster
(*Cotoneaster divaricatus*)

Stiff small leaves and strong gray stems give the *Cotoneaster* family members plenty of rugged good looks that make them a durable landscape choice across the country. But this one, spreading cotoneaster, takes the best of its relatives' good qualities and goes beyond them with outstanding red shades in three seasons. As a 6-foot hedge, it forms a thick, shiny screen with exuberant, arched branches that stand out amid more understated shrubs. But spreading cotoneaster possesses enough individual charm to stand alone at the center of a well-drained or xeriscape planting. Pink-tinged, perky white flowers start the parade in spring nestled in new leaves that look like bright green collars made just for them. As the leaves take on deeper hues, red berries bright as stop signs adorn the length of each branch all summer and fall. Not done yet, every leaf takes on deep scarlet reds that last long into fall before they finally drop. Tough as nails in sun or part shade with well-drained soils, spreading cotoneaster seldom needs any attention from its gardener once it is established. Even pruning is not recommended, except rarely, so its natural vigor can grow unrestrained with huge numbers of flowers and berries.

Zones 4–7

Blue Mist Shrub
(*Caryopteris × clandonensis*)

Clear purple-blues—cool, calming, and serene—can be hard to find in the heat of late summer gardens. Blue mist shrub solves this dilemma with subtle shades that have big impact in a shrub bed or as a featured player among perennial plants. Its flowers are packed in a cloud that can be sweet sky blue or vibrant purple, depending on the individual plant as well as its selections and cultivars. Their hues may remind you of the lavenders your great aunt favors, but there is nothing demure about this plant. The little blooms reach out in bunches from the leaf axils of stiff stems, poking above gray-green leaves that form a dense plant that is very attractive to bees and butterflies. The oddly fragrant plants form exuberant mounds about 3 feet tall and wide, and they keep their neat shape in sunny sites with well-drained soils. Blue mist blooms on new growth and will have more flowers if you cut its stems back early in spring. When a plant is named for prestigious public gardens, you can trust that it is beloved, like 'Blue Kew' and 'Longwood Blue'. Both are prized for their dark violet-blue flowers. 'Worcester Gold' harkens to another common name, blue spirea; its lavender blue flowers and yellow-green leaves make it a seasonal focal point like its namesake.

Zones 6–9

French Hybrid Ceanothus
(*Ceanothus × delilianus*)

When you first see this shrub, it's as if a new shade was invented just for your pleasure. Take the prettiest lilac and infuse it with pure purple to get a shade of lavender-blue that can be almost gray at times and is always eye-catching. These selections and cultivars show dependable blues: 'Gloire de Versailles' in lighter hues and 'Henri Desfosse' with deeper violets. French hybrid ceanothus ranges from 4 to 12 feet tall with a spreading form that provides plenty of leaf tips to hold the flower clusters that all but block out the leaves when the plants are in bloom. But the bottle green, glossy leaves carry the rest of the year with style. They are slightly coarse in texture with pronounced veins that look almost puckered; their impact is strong and separates them from other evergreen (or semievergreen) shrubs.

Other ceanothus cultivars deserve attention for color and cultural concerns. 'Dark Star' (*C.* × *'Dark Star'*) is a hybrid with dense flower cover in deep purple blue shades. *Ceanothus × pallidus* has more cold tolerance and can be grown in Zones 6 and 7. Its cultivars 'Roseus' and 'Marie Simon' offer rosy-lilac colors in dense flower clusters on shrubs 3 to 4 feet tall and wide.

Zone 8–9

Meyer Lilac
(*Syringa meyeri*)

If you think it's old-fashioned to love lilacs, you'd be correct—so long as you know that retro is *very* now. Meyer lilac is a hands-down perfect purple with no competition for looks and fragrance. Hypnotic describes this particular lilac's effect on garden visitors. You smile as the perfume finds them first and leads them to the neat, compact shrub where they marvel at how many flowers burst from each cluster. Purple tubes that define "lilac" in pastel chalks open their ends to release that heady aroma and reveal light shades inside. The combination creates colorful visual depth that obscures the leaves from view for weeks. Meyer lilac is more compact in its habit than other lilacs, with grass green leaves that are rounded and almost cupped, in smart contrast to the bubbly blooms. This one is seldom leggy, with plenty of leaves from ground level up to form a rounded shape no more than 6 feet wide and somewhat shorter. Dwarf Korean lilac (*S. meyeri* 'Palibin') is popular for its smaller overall size with plentiful flowers and compact canopy of cute little leaves. Tinkerbelle (cultivar name of 'Bailbelle') is a captivating Meyer lilac with pink buds and dark wine-colored blossoms. None are picky plants and are grown widely in their zones.

Zones 4–7

Oregon Grapeholly
(*Mahonia aquifolium*)

Some plants are intriguing to look at because they seem made of disparate parts. Even the name of this *Mahonia* can be confusing since it is not a grape nor a holly, and it is native to Oregon but also more of the Pacific Northwest. A treasure for color in the shade garden, Oregon grapeholly has leaves so green that they are blue and develop beautiful bronzy purple color in winter. This oddball shrub has crazy, spiky, scalloped leaf edges rather like some hollies and creates welcome coarse texture amid hardy ferns and azaleas. Oregon grapeholly is a devil among those angels—stiff, upright canes with spiny leaves and a cocky attitude to go with them. But it can also join other evergreens in a partly sunny hedgerow without losing any of its color punch. Tiny yellow flowers cascade in long clusters from the top of the canes each spring like bold necklaces. Soon the jewel blue fruits appear, sometimes delft blue and sometimes closer to navy, but always exquisite. And yes, the clusters *do* resemble tiny grapes in a way, yet they have a distinct presence that cannot be confused with any other plant. Both standard and dwarf varieties bring outstanding color in four seasons.

Zones 4–9

Purple Beautyberry
(*Callicarpa dichotoma*)

Like a farmer named Mr. Green, when "purple" and "beauty" are in your name, you'd better be good. This shrub lives up to its name. Purple beautyberry spends each summer putting on its sparkling berries, or drupes, in tight clusters at each leaf axil. The metallic purple berries look like BBs that have been painted and hot-glued into bundles for some ignoble purpose. The sight of them atop perfect rows of bright green leaves in late summer is enchanting, but they really pop once the leaves turn yellow most autumns. Soon you get the pleasure of watching birds devour them on a bright afternoon; the gray stems hold your interest all winter. In northern zones, you are advised to cut the stems down in late winter to stimulate new growth. Elsewhere, only minimal early spring pruning will be needed. At 4 feet tall and slightly wider, this shrub offers white, pink, or lilac flowers on a sweetly draping vase shape. It thrives with well-drained soil in partly shady to partly sunny sites and needs only minimal maintenance.

American native beautyberry (*C. americana*) is a denizen of the woods in the Southeast and is well suited to large, shady gardens.

Zones 5–8

Purple Giant Filbert

(*Corylus maxima* var. *purpurea*)

This plant needs another name as this one is misleading at best and possibly even insulting to the Filbert family. The common name implies an odd-colored, huge nut—a filbert—but you'd have to look hard for any here, and they'd be a disappointment to crack. In this case, "purple giant" refers to the extraordinary leaves of this plant, which, like other big shrubs that can be used as small trees when lower limbs are exposed, allowing a canopy to form. Gray trunks are obscured by a host of purple leaves that are fat ovals with thick veination. The waffling is strangely attractive with rough, muscular, yet still friendly good looks. Spring brings in the bold, almost metallic purple leaves; it is impossible to miss purple giant filbert even at the back of the border or in the far corner of the garden. There it does double duty with unparalleled color and a densely leafed thicket that is ideal for birds and other wildlife to rest and nest. Averaging 10 feet tall and wide but capable of larger size, this thub grows in sun or part shade where its colors stay stronger as summer wears on. Its fruits and male catkins are quite purple too.

Zones 4–8

Redleaf Loropetalum

(*Loropetalum chinense* var. *rubrum*)

There may be no more startling shrub than redleaf loropetalum. Its leaves are unmatched for pert rounded shapes and shades of deep wine shades of burgundy, merlot, and claret. They flow along every curving branch of the shrub, so perfect and plentiful they might have been piped on by a talented cake decorator. Flowers appear in spring to reinforce the color palette with fuchsia, carmine, or raspberry narrow petals that twist and flare out like shiny ribbons. A member of the witch hazel family and related to that old Southern favorite, white fringe flower, redleaf loropetalum outshines the rest of its clan with vigor that often belies its label. The species and some selections from it can reach 8 feet tall and make excellent weeping tree forms or espaliers. Some of the group go through leaf color changes while others pop out in their strong purple shades and stay that way all year. Cultivars and selections of note include 'Blush' with brilliant red flowers and rosy new growth that appears all summer to create a patchwork quilt of color; 'Garnet Fire', aptly named for its leaf color and bright red blooms; and 'Zhuzhou Fuchsia' for the deepest maroon leaves and dark pink flowers.

Zones 7–9

Sweetshrub

(*Calycanthus floridus*)

Red shades in the burgundy-maroon range of purple get plenty of attention in the fall garden, but few spring and summer flowers sport such muscular tones. Sweetshrub (or Carolina allspice) blooms with ironic beauty, in the deepest hues of purple with petals that seem sharp and stiff, as if to cut you if you dare to touch them. Their fragrance seems heaven-sent, too sweet for this tough flower orb. Their aroma is like the best fruit salad you ever smelled, a combination of banana and strawberry with pineapple and, some say, passionfruit. It lingers in the air like perfume, long enough to make you wonder about its source. In garden and vase, these flowers are unusual, tightly formed like little roses that might have been carved instead of grown in the back garden and picked days ago. Glossy leaves cover this shapely but rather squat shrub that is usually 6 to 8 feet tall and slightly wider. Sweetshrub is a native American plant that thrives in most soils including clays, and in sun or some shade where its form is more open and graceful. But in sun, there will be more flowers and brighter fall colors of gold and purple before they drop to reveal dark purple-gray stems.

Zones 4–9

Dyer's Greenwood

(*Genista tinctoria*)

It's true that good things sometimes come in small packages, and Dyer's greenwood packs plenty of bright yellow onto small, deciduous shrubs. The individual blooms and late summer seedpods give away its relations to the peas, beans, and brooms, but this shrub is more upscale than most of that family. Dyer's greenwood stacks pea-like flowers in clusters that stand erect, opening from bottom to top. Each bud is longer than wide, quite plump, and opens like a mouth ready to shout about spring's joys. Their plentiful flower spikes point straight up and cover the low mounding shrubs like birthday candles for a centenarian. The effect is dazzling in the main bloom cycle, but the flowers keep on coming sporadically for many more weeks. Dyer's greenwood gets its name from the green twigs that cover the 3-by-3-foot shrub in winter. It thrives in sunny sites, including those with poor fertility and relatively dry conditions, such as in front of fences and along sidewalks where bed preparation is impractical. 'Royal Gold' has flowers in darker gold hues on a 2-foot-tall shrub. 'Bangle' shows more heat and drought tolerance in a similar sized shrub.

Zones 4–7

Forsythia
(*Forsythia* × *intermedia*)

The first to bloom in many gardens and a welcome sight to the winter-weary, forsythia might have invented yellow flowers. The shrub is flamboyant, vase-shaped, and covered in sometimes-fragrant single or semi-double flowers on leafless stems. They grow exuberantly, all yellow arms flung wide to embrace the coming of spring. The leaves emerge kelly green and some deepen their hues in summer; they are pointed ovals with slightly serrated edges. Forsythia can be described as a vase- or funnel-shaped, and their shape is best maintained with pruning after flowering since the shrub blooms on old wood. Fall color varies but can be deep gold with exquisite purple mottling. Like many species, forsythia has given rise to many "children" in the form of cultivars, selections, and hybrids, including *Forsythia* × *intermedia*. Out of hundreds tested, a few rise to the top for the color and panache of the parents in a smaller shrub. 'Sunrise' is as wide as it is tall at 5 feet by 5 feet; dwarf 'Golden Peep' spreads across the soil with single blooms (2 feet by 3 feet); 'Mindor' or 'Show Off' is about 4 feet by 4 feet and branches freely from its vase shape for even more flowers than most; 'Meadowlark' is noted for cold tolerance.

Zones 4–8

Fothergilla
(*Fothergilla major* 'Mt. Airy')

When a hybrid plant occurs without human effort, and it is honestly better than either of its parents, you can see it as proof that nature continues to amaze. 'Mount Airy' fothergilla was named by Dr. Michael Dirr for the Ohio arboretum where he found it, the overlooked offspring of two native species. Before this deciduous shrub drops its leaves each autumn, 'Mt. Airy' simply stuns viewers with yellow and orange with red-purple tones in its fall color. It is a player in the color game in spring and summer, too, beginning with flared oval leaves 3 to 4 inches long that are bottle green with grayish blue undersides. Late spring flowers are perky bottlebrushes made of sweet-smelling, tiny flowers that pop from every stem. The flowers are white and airy, so light you can see the green stems inside brushes up to 3 inches tall and round like lollipops. They can tolerate some shade as long as the soil is moist and richly organic. One parent, *F. major*, is larger than 'Mt. Airy' and brings more apricot color to the fall show. Another, *F. gardenii*, is smaller and often called dwarf fothergilla. For added color dimension, consider 'Blue Mist' and 'Blue Shadow' fothergilla shrubs with serious blue tones in their leaves.

Zones 5–8

Fragrant Sumac
(Rhus aromatica)

Also known as lemon sumac, this shrub's colors recommend it for space in mixed hedgerows and naturalized plantings. Fall sends its neatly lobed leaflets into flaming shades of orange, yellow, and red to warm up your garden as well it does in native stands. With such bright leaves and shiny red berries gathered into tight clusters, fragrant sumac looks dressed up for every autumn celebration. A dense, deciduous thicket of stems supports all this color and more, including stacks of rounded yellowish flower clusters in spring. Their shade is subtle, yet stands out amid the pinks that can dominate gardens early in the year. Fragrant sumac spreads underground to form its spreading clump, a favorite resting place for wildlife in summer under the shade of fragrant, green to greenish yellow leaves. This shrub varies in size but is usually grown 3 feet × 4 feet or slightly larger and is pruned after flowering to shape its growth. It thrives in well-drained, even slightly rocky soils, in full sun or slightly less. The sweet flowers attract butterflies as well as other nectar-seekers, and the berries bring in hungry birds fueling up for the winter.

Although the leaves are a similar shape to the toxic sumac, none of fragrant sumac's plant parts are poisonous.

Zones 4–9

Japanese Kerria
(Kerria japonica)

A treasure introduced to Western garden culture around 1800 from Japan, the species *Kerria* is named for its collector, William Kerr. The most beautiful of the bunch by most estimation is also known as Japanese rose or 'Pleniflora', referring to its family origins and abundant double flowers. They are bright golden yellow, quarter-sized, and a rare treat in partial shade where they bloom their heads off in late winter and spring, depending on location. The outstanding flowers dot stiff, spring green stems that hold that bright hue all year long. The leaves are equally bright green, very toothy, sometimes arrow-shaped, and a bit puckered. Its linear form presents best in a bed of shrubs with contrasting shapes where it can stand out as it should. The colors and attitude of Japanese kerria are as festive as the T-shirts at a St. Patrick's Day parade. Select cultivars are slightly smaller with more predictable forms and are well suited for smaller gardens. 'Albescens' has flowers more creamy than yellow with jaunty petals that are not all alike. 'Golden Guinea' has larger, single yellow flowers. 'Simplex' offers bright yellow blooms that look more like kerria's relatives in the rose family.

Zones 4–9

Tangerine Cinquefoil

(*Potentilla fruticosa*)

When you want a shrub with impossibly large flowers to contrast with fine-textured leaves, think shrubby cinquefoil. But when you want sunny yellow blooms with touches of bright tangerine-orange, know that tangerine cinquefoil is for you. With a bloom season that lasts from late spring to fall and a preference for dry sites, it's a star that shines where few others can thrive. The shrub is wider than it is tall, usually 2 to 3 feet tall by 4 feet wide, with dusky, almost gray-green leaves that are oddly ferny in appearance. Tangerine cinquefoil is at its best with room to spread, but it is not particular about soil type so long as it drains well. Blooms will be paler yellow in full afternoon sun, and the shrub's form will be denser and, ironically, less attractive. Best used in masses, tangerine cinquefoil can line a walk, fill a flowerbed, or bloom like crazy in front of taller evergreens. Other cinquefoils have a place in modern garden design to provide low-maintenance plants with abundant flowers and interesting leaves that attract butterflies, but usually not deer. The species has pale yellow flowers with prominent centers; they are not as cupped as tangerine and other cultivars.

Zones 4–7

Witch Hazel

(*Hamamelis vernalis*)

Just when it seems that winter will go on forever, witch hazel blooms to reassure us that spring will come. In full sun or part shade, its fragrant and unusual yellow flowers burst out around the bare branches. The twisted petals flare out from dark red calyxes in delightfully whimsical, thin yellow ribbons that last for weeks in cold weather. They look like brilliant yellow spiders with many more than eight legs crawling along each stem. Such unusual color and habit in the coldest months is a welcome sight soon followed by bright green leaves that cover the grayish red stems. Witch hazel leaves seem to mirror the flowers with golden yellow fall color in most years. Native habitat is often the areas along stream beds and gravel soils where witch hazel's suckering habit can take over the space. In the garden, plant it in full sun for best flowering and in well-drained soil; prune after flowering to shape and remove suckers when they appear to control its spread. Another native, common witch hazel (*H. virginiana*) is a large shrub or small tree that blooms in late fall with yellow flowers in softer shades. Because of its astringent properties, it is used in commercial skin-care products.

Zones 4–9

Chinese Juniper

(*Juniperus chinensis*)

The name Chinese juniper has become almost generic for shrubs with blue-green needles. It has spawned scores of named cultivars and selections that are beautiful, durable, and colorful. For a range of green shades few other groups can match, fine texture, and dense form, the Chinese junipers are unrivaled in the shrub world. The light brown cones are fleshy, small, and almost round; on female junipers, they offer nubby contrast to the rich foliage colors. Chinese junipers can be trees or very large shrubs, but smaller ones and the groundcover forms are better suited for most gardens. Each depends primarily upon its color to distinguish it. 'Pfitzer Compacta' junipers are perhaps the best known, recognized by grayish sage green leaves and branches at 45-degree angles that seem to drip their needles like candlewax. 'Pfitzer Aurea' starts golden yellow in spring before its strong green takes over. 'Pfitzer Glauca' brings muted blue tones and softer texture to this classic landscape form. 'Sea Green' might have been called the mint juniper to best describe its color. About 4 feet tall and wider, its branches arch gracefully. Another 'Glauca' with very blue needles is in the × *sargentii* group of Chinese junipers, noted for ground-hugging form.

Zones 4–9

Evergreen Euonymus

(*Euonymus japonicus*)

Every garden needs go-to shrubs with dark green color that can take whatever the seasons bring. You might use them to mark an entrance or establish hedging, but the best, including this one, offer contrasting greens as foils to lighter shades. Evergreen euonymus fills these gaps, but those who have only seen the sometimes-garish variegated version may hesitate. Deep shades of bottle green and slightly lighter new growth let these leaves glow in a very good way. Rounded with slight points on the ends, evergreen euonymus leaves are held tight and dense on their stems and are so glossy they seem dipped in wax. The plants grow into fat, slightly rounded forms with a natural grace that is often concealed by the box shapes into which they are usually pruned. Delightful flowers appear on these looser shapes, whitish yellow blooms that soon form pink structures with orange seeds inside. Evergreen euonymus has other good qualities to recommend it: simple maintenance needs, adaptability to most soils, salt- and shade-tolerance, and fast response to pruning rank are among them. The pest issues common to *Euonymus* usually manifest in crowded, unpruned shrubs and are easily addressed. If variegation or a mix is needed, seek out 'Silver King' for pale green leaves with creamy white edges.

Zones 4–9

Fatsia
(Fatsia japonica)

Any garden spot in shade, part shade, or morning sun can benefit from the yellow-green hues on display in fatsia. This quirky evergreen shrub delivers coarse tropical texture in big, shiny leaves. They are palmate, or hand-shaped, and might belong to the Incredible Hulk if he had two extra thumbs. Leaf colors range from deep avocado shades in the older leaves to nearly chartreuse new growth. Each is held stiffly on a stubby stem in lighter hues that increase the bold look and visual appeal of the shrub. What starts as a fat clump of leaves near ground level soon develops a rough trunk that is dark green with brownish gray-netted patterns reminiscent of cantaloupe rinds. The trunk is more exposed as the shrub sheds lower leaves with age and adds bold notes to fatsia's tropical presence. Its greens are uncommon and expressed in unforgettable form, but this shrub explodes in late winter with light green flowers that turn creamy white. Balls of flowers stick out of their clusters on stiff stems, like unbelievably cute, fuzzy golf balls stuck on toothpicks. They attract bees in droves, adding needed nectar at a time of the year when little is available.

Zones 7–9

Heavenly Bamboo
(Nandina domestica and cultivars)

This plant lives up to its status as an exotic, both in origin and garden impact. *Nandina* was imported from Asia and got its common names, heavenly or sacred bamboo, from two of its features. The multi-stemmed shrub grows on segmented woody canes that are reminiscent of slender bamboo stems. Its rich forest green leaves are compound leaflets that form fine-textured, graceful arrow shapes. They extend horizontally from the canes like open fingers; those with the finest cut leaves look like feathers. Where they are not evergreen, fall color is red so dark it might be purple. Two dwarf nandinas set the mood where smaller plants are preferred: 'Harbor Belle' has new growth in shades of pink crowned by small white flowers in spring, followed by red berries, and 'Flirt' shines with new growth throughout the season in shades from coral-red to scarlet above dark green mature growth. The species has become invasive in some areas, but some recommended cultivars offer a neater habit and very colorful leaves. Fall color ranges from greenish yellow to orange-red and fire engine red in 'Firepower'; bushy 'Gulf Stream' has coppery-orange new growth; and smaller 'Harbour Dwarf' is wider than tall with orange and orange-bronze fall color.

Zones 6–9

Japanese Pieris
(Pieris japonica)

Some shrubs are meant for center stage, and Japanese pieris is a star, glossy as porch paint and just as slick. Its leaves are narrow, about 2 inches long, and arranged in whorls so they appear as stacked wheels around their branches. New growth is dazzling: bright, truly spring green plus coppery shades of bronze and red. The green tones deepen and the others hold as more new leaves emerge, and the big shrub becomes an organic kaleidoscope of color. At the end of a path, around a corner, Japanese pieris lights up the shade garden with a dense, rounded form. Then it blooms with draping chains of urn-shaped white flowers whose fragrance draws you in. About 8 feet tall and wide, the greens of Japanese pieris are unmatched as focal point plants but they are also dramatic in groups. Three plants in a row can create a wall of Granny Smith, emerald, and forest green in color shades. Himalayan pieris (*P. formosana* var. *forrestii*) may seem misnamed since it thrives in warmer zones, but it is well worth consideration there. It adds to the color palette with new red growth that changes to cream before becoming green, and its chains of white flowers are stunning.

Zones 5–8

Sasanqua
(Camellia sasanqua)

Hands down the best evergreen shrub for its zones, sasanqua has shiny, small (2 to 3 inch) leaves that seem unfazed, aloof from the world. Some are the rich green of Wellington boots while other varieties are as dark as champagne bottles. They do not suffer wind damage, shake off snow and ice, and laugh at summer heat. Sasanquas are not bulletproof, but their perfect green leaves surely seem to be. A denser shrub with more spectacular fall flowers is readily maintained with annual pruning after bloom season. Sasanqua varieties are chosen for their size and flower color. Standard sasanquas stand 8 to 10 feet tall and almost as wide. A favorite is 'Yuletide' with a red flower and prominent gold stamens that blooms late season. 'Kanjiro' has rose pink blooms, while 'Jean May' has small, pale pink blooms. Midsized varieties at 4 to 6 feet include the classic white 'Mine-No-Yuki' (white dove), 'Shishi Gashira' with rose pink flowers, and sweet pink 'Showa-No-Sakae'. Dwarf varieties include 'Marge Miller' that grows 1 foot tall with a weeping form and pink flowers, and 'Chansonette', which matures at 2 to 3 feet with rose pink flowers.

Zones 7–9 (marginal at Zone 6)

Summersweet

(*Clethra alnifolia*)

Summer in the garden can be almost monochrome green, with only a few subtle differences in leaf color and texture to distinguish one green plant from others. Summersweet bucks that trend to stand out with dynamic pea shades arranged on an upright, open form in shady spaces. The thin leaves pick up any breeze in a pleasing lilt, but this American native and its cultivars make you wait for their lighthearted garden impact. The long, narrow leaves sometimes turn darker but often maintain lighter shades all summer in much needed, finer-textured contrast to the neighboring shrubs. An inch wide and up to 4 inches long, the leaves take on creamy yellow colors in fall, a welcome feature in a thicketing shrub form like this one. New suckers can be left to spread, cut down to control their size, or dug up and transplanted. Sweetshrub tops its sparkling form with fragrant flower spikes that may be pink or white and are more plentiful in sunnier sites. Larger, smaller, and different color sweetshrubs deserve consideration. 'Pink Spires' reaches 8 to 10 feet tall, while 'Hummingbird' will be compact and no larger than 4 feet. For darker green leaves, red flower buds, and deep pink blossoms, 'Ruby Spice' is a favorite selection.

Zones 4–9

Adam's Needle Yucca

(*Yucca filamentosa*)

A clump of strappy, rather sticky leaves with sharp pointy ends and odd peeling hairs sounds like a Halloween scarecrow, not a desirable shrub. Yet Adam's needle yucca is a true garden treat beloved for towering poles of perfect summer white flowers that attract butterflies in droves. The leaves can be 3 feet long, lower ones splayed out on the ground and the rest upright, sounding a bold textural note in the garden. They are trombones, not trumpets, and demand attention for beautiful contrast to almost every other plant. The leaves may be green, blue-green, or variegated with yellow, all perfect foils for the wistfully creamy white flower stalks that rise from them each year. Adam's needle blooms are puffy orbs stacked up like marshmallows on thick stalks often taller than the 3-foot shrub. At first sight, the two parts seem oddly juxtaposed, yet the total effect is pleasing, ruggedly handsome, and quite welcome in contemporary gardens. Native to much of the US, the colors of both leaves and flowers on Adam's needle are most pronounced in full sun but it tolerates some shade and needs only minimal water once established.

Zones 4–9

Annabelle Hydrangea
(*Hydrangea arborescens* 'Annabelle')

Sometimes a species gives rise to a plant so superior to its parent that you marvel that they are related. Smooth leaf hydrangea (*H. arborescens*) is nondescript in nature, but steps up in the garden and, happily, its daughter is a real show-off. Luscious, huge flower heads in late spring make Annabelle the finest hydrangea in the family for bright white color that lasts weeks. At their best, the flowers can be as big as basketballs, so large it seems they might break the branches that hold them. What you see are scores of white bracts that surround tiny flowers, packed tightly together in stunning clusters on sturdy shrubs often wider than they are tall. The bracts age, turning pale green and then tan whether you leave them on the shrub or deadhead them. Removing old flowers often brings on more blooms for a double feature of lush white flowers later in the summer. Once they are gone, Annabelle shifts to fall color and maintains your interest with large serrate leaves that turn delicious shades of yellow, especially in southern zones. Whether in sun or part shade, Annabelle hydrangea can be pruned each spring to shape and keep its new growth dense to display the magnificent flowers.

Zones 4–9

Chinese Fringe Flower
(*Loropetalum chinense*)

A favorite in cottage gardens and older landscapes, Chinese fringe flower has robust, somewhat open form and cascades of ribbony white flowers. This shrub is attractive year-round, just waiting to herald summer with curly white streamers that seem made for the season: they are as cool as coconut gelato. Reliable in part shade or dappled sun, Chinese fringe flower tickles the air, and its motion draws you closer to see the flowers in detail. They remind you of witch hazel blooms, and both are in the same plant family; that's why Chinese fringe flower is sometimes called Chinese witch hazel. Fast-growing, it can reach 10 feet tall and be pruned into a small tree, but it is far superior as a large, rather effusive presence in the garden maintained at about 6 to 8 feet wide and tall. Fringe flower's rounded leaves are dark green with darker veins, average 2 inches long, and emerge alternately along gently arched branches. They are nearly evergreen; new leaves come on as old ones drop off. This shrub was introduced to the United States from Asia in the late nineteenth century, long before its red-leafed relative made its debut, and continues to deliver cooling color to the summer garden.

Zones 7–9

Chinese Photinia
(*Photinia serrulata*)

The *Photinia* family has gotten a bad name since its standout, Fraser photinia (*P. fraseri*), was besieged by leaf spot disease. Thankfully, there are others waiting to step up with even more colorful features and no fungus issues. Chinese photinia brings evergreen leaves with sawtooth edges that put on new growth with the trademark reddish shades. But these clusters have creamy bronze tones that add colorful, desirable bulk to these big, round, coarse-textured shrubs each year. Puffy and hairy, the warm white flower clusters stand out in late spring in a stark contrast to the dark green older leaves and bronzy new ones. Scores of small blossoms join forces in flat, jaunty flower heads that sit like a Sunday-best hat atop every branch tip. The creamy flowers have a distinct smell and hold great attraction for pollinating insects in search of breakfast. Soon berries form that slowly turn to bright red in fall, a feature seldom seen on the Frasers. Another evergreen relative, oriental photinia (*P. villosa*), has creamy white flowers with impressive red berries and fall color in yellow and orange hues. Both can be trained into small trees, but their landscape value is greater as large shrubs used for colorful hedging and screens.

Zones 5–9

Glossy Abelia
(*Abelia × grandiflora*)

There are gaps in the color palette of every garden and, white summer- and fall-flowering shrubs fall right into those. Glossy abelia takes on that challenge not only with late-season blooms but also with attractive features the rest of the year. A prize in sun or part shade, abelia forms an upright fountain of thin branches that spills wider than it is tall. The leaves are glossy bottle green, neatly pointed, and plentiful; they turn rich bronze and coppery in autumn. In warmer zones the shrubs are evergreen or nearly so but even where the leaves drop entirely, they persist well into fall and then reveal the fine lines of their supporting thicket. Spring's new growth has a rosy glow until the leaves unfurl; trimming it then resets the process for more colorful tips. Blooms appear on the current year's wood from early summer until after Labor Day. Each one is a little white trumpet standing on a rosy ring of sepals and held in sumptuous clusters. They are sweetly fragrant and a welcome nectar source for late in the season. Hedges and mixed beds welcome abelias, and the small variety 'Little Richard' makes a fine container plant.

Zones 6–9 (marginal at Zone 5)

Pearlbush

(*Exochorda racemosa*)

Selecting shrubs that bloom before their leaves emerge in spring speaks volumes about your innermost desires. They shout the sentiment, "C'mon already, it's time for the season to change!" Few carry the message better than pearlbush, also called common pearlbush although there is nothing low-class about this shrub. Its flower buds do look like perfect white pearls and as they open, cupped white flowers open in succession from bottom to top on 6-inch raceme clusters. They spill out from myriad branches that grow their own way in a loose form about 10 feet high and wide that is perfect to display the flowers. Planted in a shrub border or as a backdrop to perennials, pearlbush dazzles early and then puts on handsome small, medium-green leaves in a perky, if somewhat unpredictable form. Light pruning after the flowers finish keeps pearlbush in its space, unless you prefer its naturally wilder, offbeat shape. Fall color varies depending on location but is generally muted. 'The Bride' joins this species and another *Exochorda* to create a smaller shrub about 4 feet tall and slightly wider. Its branches arch sweetly to show off lots of smaller flowers in 4-inch racemes.

Zones 4–8

Slender Deutzia

(*Deutzia gracilis* and cultivars)

Splendid white flowers are the icing on the cake of these flamboyant *Hydrangea* relatives, slender deutzia and her cultivar offspring. All have scores of sweet-smelling, bell-shaped blooms in spring that are held in loose clusters called racemes. In sunny, well-drained garden soil, they cover the shrub, and bees cover them in a breathtaking spectacle. The plants are generally round with narrow branches that arch gracefully yet have the strength to withstand the wildest storms. They are durable, low-maintenance shrubs that can be 5 feet tall and as wide. Lance-shaped and dark green, the deciduous leaves sit opposite one another along the stems, adding to its graceful garden impact. Smaller than the species, two cultivars have additional features that offer design uses beyond the classic mixed hedgerow. Award-winning 'Nikko' soon reaches 2 feet tall and spreads slowly to 5 feet wide, perfect for spilling over a garden wall. Its flower bells have showy yellow stamens. *Deutzia* 'Duncan', whose trade name is Chardonnay Pearls, has lime-yellow leaves all year on a slightly larger shrub. It holds its flowers in tiny fists; the effect is round, rather like pearls. Popular in cottage gardens since the early twentieth century, showy deutzia (*D.* × *magnifica*) can provide 10 feet of grayish green leaves and double flowers.

Zones 5–8 (marginal at Zone 9)

Flowering perennials

Hosta 'Undulata'

Hosta plantaginea

Hosta

(*Hosta*)

Hostas, also called plantain lilies, gleam in the shade garden with clumps of wide, pointed leaves that drape like limp daggers. Plantain lily paints the scene with a range of rich green, blue, and sometimes yellow and white hues. The plants have such presence they are impossible to ignore even at a distance and glow like summer candles on the patio when they bloom. Solids, stripes, and colorful edges mark the leaves and are topped by spikes of bell-shaped, often fragrant flowers in summer. These perennials grow in richly organic, well-drained soil that has a ready water supply nearby. Some are best suited for deep shade while others do best in more light; different sizes, leaf patterns, and flower colors add even more pizazz to plantings. In general, blue leaf hybrids grow better in northern zones than they do in the South and West. 'Big Daddy' pours out waffled blue leaves and white flowers. Most unusual, 'Abiqua Drinking Gourd' has blue, quite bizarre cup-shaped leaves. An exception to the northern rule is 'Blue Angel' with huge, silvery blue leaves and white flower

bells. It thrives in light shade with consistently moist soil and is often 30 inches tall in Zones 5 through 9.

The choice of hostas is greatest in Zones 4 to 8. Green-leaved plantain lilies pack plenty of textural contrast, like 'Aphrodite' with its distinct veins and white flowers; it grows 18 inches tall and wide. Taller and wider, 'Royal Standard' offers pleasant aromas in white flowers above sharply ribbed, light green leaves.

'Bright Lights', 2 feet tall and wide, pops with lime-green leaves edged in dark blue-green and white trumpets. Two feet tall with green leaves edged in white, 'Minuteman' stops traffic with fat purple flowers. Just as large with fat, yellow-edged green leaves, 'Wide Brim' lives up to its name. 'Olive Bailey Langdon' is focal-point *big*, a yard tall and twice as wide. Her leaves are deep green with wide, pale green edges, and white flowers. Smaller but no less dramatic, 'Whirlwind' gives its leaves a quaint twist, accentuating the yellow color with green edging.

Truly impressive at nearly 4 feet tall and wide, 'Empress Wu' brings leaves in deep green with a blue cast to every zone. The flowers are lilac and borne on short stems. The whimsically named 'Night Before Christmas' has sharply pointed leaves painted white down their wide middles like Santa's beard. Its purple flowers are the perfect tubular bells.

Perennial plants create a sense of place and convey reliability when they return year after year to bloom abundantly in their season. Combining a pair of bold colors, such as this bright yellow coreopsis and blue salvia, says much about a gardener.

Copper iris

Siberian iris

Iris

(Iris spp.)

When a group of plants rings the bell for enough people, it can inspire great art as irises have for centuries. Few remember the leaves, their shafts like arrows pointing skyward, usually stiff and always sharply pointed. A bed of colorful iris can grow anywhere and reinforce your garden's signature shade in spring or summer. A clump or three in a perennial border can carry the eye from color burst to color burst. Their heights vary, adding to garden utility. Some iris plants have flower petals that hang down, known as falls, and also have additional structures on those downward petals. Those are the beards that give this group their name, but there are other important differences between this group and other irises. The bearded irises are drought-tolerant sun-lovers and require soil that is relentlessly well drained. There are six defined types of bearded iris, characterized by their height, flower size, and bloom time. When choosing bearded irises for the garden, a plant's height may determine its usefulness but flower color brings it home.

The others, the *beardless* irises, are no less interesting and include a plethora of specific kinds that are generally more tolerant of different growing conditions. They are usually more casual in style, and have narrower, more grass-like leaves that form strong clumps. Yet beardless irises present as many colors, bicolors, and fascinating flower details in endless combinations. While more exist than those listed below, these few beardless irises dominate garden culture; most bloom later than spring's earliest bearded iris.

- **Siberian iris** are divas in light shade with neat "bouquets." Flower colors include unusual orange and brown as well as purple-red, yellow, and blue.
- **Japanese iris** have been described as "corsage iris," a reference to their huge, flat shape. Their ruffles and flourishes come in blues, purples, and white with some marbling and cute yellow flecks.

Three native irises bring a sense of place:

- **LA (Louisiana) iris** show the flattest flowers with the fattest petals in every color but pure orange—and some of the reds come close, reflecting their copper iris parentage (*I. fulva*).
- **Pacific Coast iris** include 11 species native to fields and woods in milder climates along the West Coast. Flower colors range from white and yellow to pale and deep purples just short of true red.
- **Virginia iris** (*I. virginica*) may be white, blue, or lavender with elegantly simple flowers found in native meadows and at water's edge in the eastern US. They are carefree in the garden.

Mealycup sage *(S. farinacea)*

Bog sage

Salvia

(Salvia spp.)

The repetition of related plants can create color harmony and design unity—when some are taller or shorter than others, the effect is greatly reinforced. That's where salvias make their well-deserved reputation. Salvias put on dense clumps of lance-shaped leaves just stiff enough to stand out in greens from light to dark. The spectacular flower spikes are sturdy towers of flowers that attract bees, butterflies, and hummingbirds in droves. Their colors range from deep apricot and rose-red pinks to sky blue, royal blue, and a multitude of purples. From small and sweet to big, muscular stalks, the flowers have the same essential structure—a tube with an extended lower "lip." Sunny sites and areas with some shade in very hot climates, well-drained fertile soil, and moderate water are the keys to months of salvia flowers for many seasons. There are many perennial salvias to choose from; here are some that may be overlooked.

Zones 4–8:
- **Caradonna sage** (*S. nemorosa*) has sleek, dark green leaves in a foot-tall rosette topped with even taller and dramatic violet flower spikes.
- **Eveline sage** (*S.* 'Eveline') sends up ethereal lilac-lavender flowers on spikes almost 2 feet tall that dominate their light green leaves.

- **May Night sage** (*S.* × *sylvestris* 'Mainacht') is big at 20 inches tall and wider. Its dark flower stems are vivid lavender.

Zones 5–9:
- **'Texas Wedding'** (*S. greggii*) forms a clump 2 feet by 2 feet with stunning, pristine white flowers.
- **Cobalt sage** (*S. reptans*) is more upright than most with leaves like needles. The plant is 3 feet tall and spectacular with raucous blue flowers.

Zones 6–9:
- **'Pink Preference'** (*S. greggii*) is 2 feet tall and 3 feet wide with dark, rosy pink flowers that have dramatic, nearly black calyxes.
- **Furman's red sage** (*S. greggii* 'Furman's Red') has the truest red flowers on a taller plant, 3 feet by 2 feet.
- **'Maraschino'** is a *S. greggii* hybrid that reaches 3 feet tall and wider with flowers the color of red velvet cake.
- **Japanese sage** (*S. nipponica* 'Fuji Snow') is breathtaking all year. Its white leaf margins dissolve in summer, replaced by huge pastel yellow flower spikes that are more than a foot long.
- **Bog sage** (*S. uliginosa*) easily grows bigger than 4 feet tall in sunny, wet sites. The clumps are covered with a sky blue cloud of flowers for months.

Threadleaf tickseed

Largeflower tickseed

Tickseed

(*Coreopsis* spp.)

Lots of gardeners want the airy feeling of wildflowers but their design has no vast space for swaths of native perennial plants. Coreopsis brings that loose, country vibe into cultivated gardens in all zones with bright, golden yellow pops of color. Tickseed is the common name given to the entire family, and all have similar, tick-looking seeds, but there the obvious resemblance ends. Leaves range from spring green to bluish, substantial to quite thin in shape. The flowers present almost endless vamps on the classic daisy shape, and some have markings the color of redwood. Small or large, on short stems or impossibly long ones, the vast majority of flowers are buttercup yellow but some are orange, red, or pink. Tickseeds are full sun plants, happy in all but rich, wet soils; some can grow in pure sand or gravel.

Largeflower tickseed (*C. grandiflora*) is the granddaddy of the garden bunch, native and self-sowing to delight or chagrin, depending on space available for the tall plants. On plants 2 to 3 feet tall, the 2-inch blooms have greenish centers and solid, bright yellow ray petals with characteristic notched petals. **Lanceleaf tickseed** (*C. lanceolata*) sets a lighter, airy mood with finer-textured leaves on a plant about 18 to 24 inches tall. Its flowers that look more like traditional daisies, yellow petals with

dark centers. **Threadleaf tickseed** (*C. verticillata*) puts its sturdy yellow daisies with pointed petals on deceptively wimpy-looking stems and leaves. Their novelty is matched only by their reliable, colorful show on plants 24 to 30 inches tall in the species but varied in its selections. 'Zagreb' is a very small threadleaf, while 'Golden Shower' is tall and blooms for weeks. Creamy yellow, almost white, 'Moonbeam' blooms in between the others. A bed of all three puts low-maintenance, high-impact color in place to carry a happy message of welcome.

Other selections and varieties of *Coreopsis* are often named for our planet's star and their color. 'Rising Sun' shows off yellow petals with red bases in a semi-double bloom with a yellow center. Thinner leaves and a looser, more casual habit give 'Baby Sun' a showy single flower with bright red rings where the yellow petals meet their center. 'Early Sunrise' is smaller with slightly wider leaves than the species and solid yellow, semi-double blooms. A delightful red tickseed, 'Mercury Rising' is a smaller plant selected from *C. rosea* that blooms for months in Zones 5 to 8 with deep red-purple flowers on fine-textured leaf mounds.

Astilbe
(*Astilbe hybrids*)

Astilbes are shade garden staples with more colors available every year as breeders expand the palette. They range in height from 6 inches to nearly 4 feet tall, with fernlike leaves and thin, upright stems. Leaf colors range on the dark side of green, with bronze and copper overtones, to bright spring greens. Each leaf widens at its middle, tapers to a graceful point, and is toothed or scalloped on its edge. Those flowers are nothing short of spectacular, tiny flowers gathered into plumes fancy enough to adorn any Sunday chapeau. Shades of pink astilbes include salmon, coral, bubblegum, and pastel chalk. There are true reds, lavenders, purples, and whites. Bloom times vary from spring through summer, and flowers differ slightly among the diverse hybrids. Dark scarlet 'Fanal' is one of many *Astilbe × arendsii* hybrids that thrive in the shade garden with moist, organic soils. 'Federsee' (also called 'Catherine Deneuve') forms a mound of leaves 18 inches tall with rose-pink flowers on fluffy spikes that can double its height. 'Ostrich Plume' stuns with coral pink flowers in looser clusters than most. No taller than a foot in bloom, dwarf astilbes are distinctly pixie-ish and appealing. 'Key West', for example, has rich pink, tufted flowers above coppery green leaves.

Zones 4–8

Beardtongue
(*Penstemon hybrids*)

Simply beautiful pink or red flowers fill beds and big sections of many perennial borders for plenty of bells on sturdy stems. The flower tubes open with pouty lower petals and one hairy stamen, or tongue; some seem to positively smirk at you. They range in shades from carnation pink to bright and deep claret reds and can bloom for weeks in bright sunny gardens. In the warmer zones, flower color will be stronger longer if the plants are located away from late afternoon heat. Once established in well-drained soil, the plants are quite drought tolerant. Several species of *Penstemon* are native to different parts of the United States and have been bred extensively with English species to create the chic perennials we enjoy. Beardtongue hybrids include the dramatic 'Dark Towers', with purple leaves and baby pink flowers, and 'Hidcote Pink', a favorite for clear pink blooms. The flaming red of 'Ruby' flares from stems invisible under so many flowers, while 'Red Riding Hood' is bright red with a very upright growth pattern that creates an unusually regimented effect. 'Firebird' blooms traffic signal red on thin stems with strappy leaves, and the denser crown of 'Port Wine' puts up stunning flowers worthy of their name.

Zones 4–7

Cardinal Flower

(*Lobelia cardinalis*)

Up to six feet tall at its best, this is a Roman candle of a perennial plant in summer and fall. Big clumps of showy green leaves grow quickly to support tall flower spikes as scarlet as Miss O'Hara. The jade green leaves are long and narrow with prominent veins that run their length and add to the plant's graceful stance. The red flowers crown each stem with fat tubular buds that open over several days from the bottom to the flaming red tip. Nectar hides deep inside the tube, accessible to hummingbirds as they hover over the open petals whose colors attract them. Two silky, rich red upper petals are curved back and three more spread out like a welcome mat. Each is about an inch long and united in clusters called racemes that hold the colors high on the leafy stems like flags on fire. Long-lived in the vase, cardinal flower makes a great cut flower. But let some flowers go to seed to replenish the stand. Cardinal flowers take the sun in northern zones but farther south, they grow in partial shade. Richly organic soil that gets water regularly will bring on the most flowers and bring in the hummingbirds.

Zones 4–9

Columbine

(*Aquilegia canadensis*)

Romantic and demure, columbine nods its flowers on thin, rod-like stems as if it is too shy to speak. These bells speak in color, cardinal red and canary yellow, and their message is a clear welcome to the wildflower patch or partly shady garden bed. Hummingbirds are drawn to the droopy blooms that have red spurs and sepals, yellow petals and stamens arranged like elfin hats in a fairy garden. Sometimes as tall as 3 feet, columbine is most often seen as a mature plant in its second year at 18 to 24 inches in height, but often blooms in its first spring in the garden. It is not impatient to grow although the flowers will be smaller and in proportion to the young plants. The clumps are vigorous with rounded leaflets in threes that are gently scalloped and nearly lime green or slightly darker in color. As good in a naturalized design as a formal one where a low edging plant that blooms is always welcome, columbine needs rich organic soil that drains well and regular irrigation in hot summers. If allowed, it will reseed to replenish and increase its stand. Beyond that, this plant stands its ground sweetly, but with quiet resolve.

Zones 3–8 (marginal to Zone 9)

Garden Phlox
(*Phlox paniculata*)

From full-sun borders to beds in a bit of shade, garden phlox packs a color wallop for weeks if not months in spring and summer. Every shade of pink and red, some with bright red bull's eyes, paint inch-wide pinwheel flowers that are gathered into tall, fragrant flower heads. At times it seems the stems cannot possibly support such big flowers, and they do waft in the breeze a bit but seldom fall over. Flower colors include the pink blushed 'Prospero', pale pinks of 'Bright Eyes' with proper red "eyes," and 'Franz Schubert', a petite pleasure at only 3 feet tall. Rosier pinks like 'Red Eyes' and the unfortunately named 'Red Indian' are the pretty pinks of ballet shoes and tutus. But the boldest in this bunch are gaudy neon pink: 'Fairest One' with especially dense flower heads and the huge (5 feet tall) 'Robert Poore'. The plants are thick with light green leaves, pointed and jaunty on their ends, and thrive in most soils with moderate needs for water and other maintenance. The intoxicating fragrance of phlox puts the power of cloves and cottage pinks on steroids. Just one flower cluster holds its perfume in potpourris and pressed flowers long after the color has finally faded.

Zones 4–8 (marginal to Zone 9)

Peony
(*Paeonia* hybrids)

Peonies are native to southern Europe, the western United States, and Asia, but the vast majority of the ones we grow are Asian hybrids. Not every perennial flower performs as well in the vase as in the garden; peonies are stars in both places for days if not weeks of color. Green-stemmed, herbaceous clumps average 3 feet tall and 2 feet wide and need little more attention than their bedmates in the perennial border. New shoots are often red, and there are scores of pink and red flowers to be grown in a variety of flower types from single to semi- and fully doubled petal arrangements, as well as Japanese and anemone-flowered types. And if you search far and wide for corals, peony shines a warm light in that color group too. Most of the flowers are fragrant and the plants long lived in temperate zone gardens. Select local favorite peony varieties for best performance, especially in the South and West, where warm winters are the rule. Tree peonies are shrubs and not considered here except as one parent of the intersectional hybrids, also called Itoh peonies. These are hugely popular because they bloom longer with stronger stems and often huge flowers, including pink and coppery rose.

Zones 4–8 (marginal to Zone 9)

Pinks

(*Dianthus* spp. and hybrids)

The expression "pretty in pink" might have been coined for this diverse group. They are a broad bunch that includes the robust cottage pinks (*D. plumarius*) and delicate cheddar pinks, (*D. gratianopolitanus*) as well as other species and hybrids. Their colors run the gamut from palest pastel to pink shades made for Easter hats, to bright fuchsias and purplish reds. Five petals sit close together around a darker center or dark ring to create tiny saucers filled with color. Most are fragrant and bloom on stems atop gray-green mounds or mats of quill-like leaves. Well-drained soil and full sun are the keys to success with these small perennials whether along a bed's edge or filling containers of early spring color. None is taller than 18 inches and most are smaller; some spread and some form round mounds, but all are covered with flowers each spring. Scores of choices await you, including these three: 'Bath's Pink' sets the standard for cheddar pinks with the darkest leaves and brightest icy pink fringed flowers. 'Grandiflorus' has loud, rosy pink blooms that open almost flat with bright red rings in their center. 'Dad's Favorite' is a wild, multipetaled, red-and-white bicolor flower that shouts for attention.

Zones 4–8

Purple Coneflower

(*Echinacea* spp.)

Make no mistake: the traditional "purple" coneflower is *pink*. Its hues vary from almost pastel to nearly but not quite purple, but they are pink nonetheless with burgundy-brown or even orange centers. The species, *E. purpurea*, is widely grown, native to the Midwest and southeastern United States, and the source of many of the best garden selections. Its flowers are the classic "pink daisies" of cottage garden design with distinct, pointed cones that swell with seeds each summer. The plants are considered easy to grow, drought tolerant, and ideal for sunny sites including slopes. Robust and hardy, coneflower clumps are dark green with leaves shaped like arrows that take this plant straight into your heart in sun or partial shade. 'Ruby Star', commonly called Rubinstern, has only a slightly drooped flower much like the species on a more compact plant. Other outstanding coneflowers include some with exaggerated cones: 'After Midnight' with dark fuchsia petals, lighter pink 'Pixie Meadowbrite', and 'Double Decker', prized for a swingy skirt under the cone and a wacky topknot of petals above it. Closer to sheer red, 'Tomato Soup' has flowers that face you, while 'Summer Sun' starts with glowing red and changes to orange and gold in a few days.

Zones 4–8 (marginal at Zone 9)

Clematis
(*Clematis* hybrids)

Climbing around a mailbox post or clambering up a sunny trellis, blue and purple clematis vines are unmatched for colorful vigor. There are choices for every zone with spring, fall, and intermittent bloom times, but all thrive in sunny spots with shade on their roots. The interspecies hybrid Jackman clematis with its classic purple flowers is the best known for its dark shining petals that pop out from tight yellow centers. But another one, Durant's clematis, has more flowers that are only slightly smaller on a neater, dark green vine. Modern hybrids gain attention for huge, cooling blue flowers like pale 'Madame Chalmondeley', blue-purple 'Pearl d'Azure', and the lilac shades of 'Elsa Spath'. A charming hybrid feature retains blue shades in the seed heads long after the flowers are done. Nonvining clematis deserve attention for clusters of brilliant purple tube-shaped flowers. 'Cote d'Azur' and lighter colors of 'Wyevale Blue' are popular cultivars of *C. heracleifolia* popular in Zones 4 to 7. Renowned breeder Raymond Evison has turned the tables on this group with Petit Faucon (the tradename for *C.* 'Evisix') and others. Best grown as true perennials and cut down each spring at rose-pruning time, the deep metallic purple petals of Petit Faucon open with long petals amid shrub roses.

Zones 4–9

Gayfeather
(*Liatris spicata*)

You might not recognize that the flower blooming by the side of the road is the same one in that fancy bouquet from the florist. But both may be gayfeather, or blazing star, that can easily bring its colorful flower spikes to every sunny garden, too. Each little bloom looks like a tiny mauve or purple button whose shape reveals its membership in the Aster plant family. They are packed tightly along tall flower spikes in shades uncommon in summer and so are as welcome in the perennial border as they are in naturalized areas. Fluffy as a feather boa and erect as a soldier at attention, this native wildflower opens from the top down, a most unusual and whimsical habit in garden plants. The plants average about 5 feet tall and bloom in summer atop stems with wispy leaves that look frail but are not; they thrive in full sun with moist, well-drained soil. 'Kobold' is a smaller plant with brilliant flower colors on the lilac side while the flowers of 'Floristan Violett' are stunning violet blue. A relative, *Liatris graminifolia*, has equally exotic flower color in lilac-blue but with grassy leaves unlike its relatives.

Zones 4–9

Joe-Pye Weed
(*Eupatorium* spp.)

It's said that an expert is a journeyman far from home, and that adage certainly applies to Joe-pye weed. This native perennial has long been both a garden favorite overseas and a weed to be conquered at home. But if you like purple flower heads as big as footballs and shaped like them, too, this is your plant for late summer color. Stacks of pointed leaves longer than they are wide stick straight out from stems as tall as 10 feet in areas of cool summers. Thick clumps push up scads of tiny flowers in purple clouds that attract a bevy of bees and butterflies. If their height would overwhelm its bedmates, this plant and the very similar spotted Joe-pye weed (*E. maculatum*, with stems blotched purple) can be pinched in spring to shorten their ultimate height, but 'Gateway' is grown for its naturally shorter stature. Wherever you cultivate Joe-pye weed, consider adding its relative, wild ageratum (*E. coelestinum*), as a companion in the bed for complimentary flower colors. The flower clusters on these smaller plants are delicious lilac to blue shades; together they are irresistible. The entire group deserves your attention.

Zones 4–8 (marginal to Zone 9)

Speedwell
(*Veronica spicata*)

From the front edge of a border to center stage in colorful beds, speedwell finds a home in sunny perennial plantings. Blue, bluer, and bluest might describe the pointy flower spikes with clear hues that stand out in any planting. Upright and covered in buds, speedwell looks like a mass of pale green fingers pointing skyward; when they open, there is no more eye-popping sight to be seen. Beloved for its neat, dark green, toothy leaves and plentiful flowery spikes, the plants bloom for weeks in summer and then spread by rooting stems as they fall over. From less than a foot tall to more than 2 feet in full bloom, speedwell wins the blue ribbon for easy perennial color. 'Blue Fox' has lavender or lilac-blue flowers on a petite plants, and 'Glory', also known as 'Royal Candles', is noted for flowers that are dark violet. Tiny 'Nana Blauteppich' blooms bright blue at less than 4 inches tall, and 'Romiley Purple' has a muscular look and blue-violet blossoms. A subspecies, *V. incana* 'Silver Carpet', has the additional desirable feature of silver-green leaves to go with its deep blue blooms. Many gardeners recognize speedwell as the first blue flower they ever remember seeing; its potent colors are memorable.

Zones 4–8

Stokes' Aster

(Stokesia laevis)

Sometimes a native perennial plant gives rise to such stunning offspring that they far outshine the species. In fact, people may not even recognize the dainty, inch-wide light blue "daisies" with fine petals extended around a wide round center. It is a sweet, late spring-flowering doll and a good companion to small ferns and native columbine in naturalized settings. With much larger flowers, brighter colors in shades from delft blue to nearly purple, Stokes' aster daughters are ready for a debutante's ball. Their flowers are held on light green stems above the clumps and can come in waves for weeks if you deadhead them. The leaves offer bright contrast to the flowers with strappy, almost lime green color piled into thick clumps. They thrive in sunny to partly shady sites where soils are well drained in all but the most northern zones where they can be enjoyed as container plants. The most popular, *Stokesia* 'Blue Danube', lives up to its name with clear blue blooms 2 to 3 inches wide. 'Wyoming' delivers deeper purple tones while 'Klaus Jelitto' brings even larger blue flowers on plants that can be 2 feet tall in bloom. 'Omega Skyrocket' has erect stems and is perfect for the cut flower garden.

Zones 5–9

Black-Eyed Susan

(Rudbeckia spp., hybrids, and cultivars)

Step into the world of black-eyed Susan flowers for unmistakable, bold color that shines up at you in big daisy shapes surrounding deep, dark centers. Flower shades range from orange coneflower (*R. fulgida*) to the lemony yellow petals of cutleaf coneflower (*R. laciniata*) with dozens of selections and hybrids in between. The flower petals simply glow with vibrant, heartwarming color whether one plant or a plethora comes into view. The colors have tremendous depth that shines through in every photo, even those taken with the simplest camera. Black-eyed Susans are at home in full sun, and most adapt to any average soil but are less tolerant of severe drought conditions. By far the most popular, 'Goldsturm' calls on its sturdy *R. fulgida* background with golden yellow petals around a dark disk 3 inches across. Fast to grow and colonize, the plants easily reach 2 feet tall and wide or larger and dominate their space if allowed. Slightly less rambunctious but sunnier yellow with a small, dark nose, *R. hirta* readily reseeds itself. Double-flowered black-eyed Susans are as easy to grow and make excellent cut flowers, including 'Goldquelle' that looks like a buttery yellow chrysanthemum. It is a treasure for zones with cool summers.

Zones 3–8 (marginal to Zone 9)

Blanket Flower
(*Gallardia* spp. and hybrids)

Many plants seem to get their common names from their beautiful blooms, perhaps none as appropriately as blanket flower. The name speaks volumes once you have seen it, but read closely. While you might associate the colors and patterns of fiery yellow, gold, and red that mark blanket flower with the beautiful blankets woven by Native Americans, the plant is named for its spreading habit. Some creep across the sand in coastal zones, others spread into tall stands on the prairies, and smaller selections add to small pots. All deserve more attention in sunny garden spots for their crazy colors in striking patterns. Blanket flowers bred for garden culture mostly come from *G. × grandiflora* and include 'Goblin' with petals that are orange-red with golden tips on a foot tall plant. 'Tokajer' can be 2 feet tall and brings raucous rusty-orange flowers (with a tinge of purple). The 'Lollipop' series of blanket flowers look like their name—stiff stems hold the double orange flowers high above the dense, hairy clump of leaves. Another blanket flower, *G. aristata*, is native across the northern tier to the West Coast. From it comes 'Bijou', noted for 3-inch-wide, rich orange-red flowers with golden notes on plants no more than a foot tall.

Zones 4–9

Daylily
(*Hemerocallis*)

When a youngster picks a bouquet, enthusiasm sometimes wins and nary a blossom is spared. Mothers can relax and smile when daylily stems are clutched tight in little fists—new buds will open again tomorrow. Indeed, everywhere you look in late spring and summer daylilies of a dozen types bloom, many with the sunniest yellows, most brilliant golds, and the orangiest oranges in the garden. More than any other plant group, our beloved daylilies can be bred in every direction: single and double flowers, dwarf and giant plants, rebloomers, and the tongue-twisting diploids and tetraploids. Petals may be solid shades or bi- or tricolored, but many modern daylilies are the children of the big, tawny orange *H. fulva*; the golden *H. dumortieri*; and the smaller, lemon yellow *H. minor*. Among hundreds of named choices, the legendary 'Mary Todd' holds its own for pure deep yellow; equally storied are 'Hyperion' and 'Lemon Drop'. Dwarf and reblooming 'Stella d'Oro' introduced daylilies to container culture. Another old favorite, 'Kwanzo', has no rivals for double orange flowers. Full sun in almost any soil grows long, narrow leaves into robust clumps ready to send up lots of stems with flowers that each last but one glorious day.

Zones 4–9

Sundrops
(Oenothera fruiticosa)

Like another common name in this family, evening primrose, sundrops is the moniker given to many plants unrelated to it. The "true" sundrops bloom all day with bright, crayon-yellow flowers that have four fat, papery petals on perky stems above plants about 20 inches tall. But hybrids born of marriages with pink evening primroses may open late in the day like them; nevertheless, sundrop yellows embody the positive outlook that defines the color. Its buds are often pink with red stems and pink or red flower parts, but you can be forgiven for not noticing them once the screaming yellow flowers open. 'Sonnenwende' makes the most dramatic bicolor statement with rosy pink buds, but its yellow flowers are the attraction. 'Lady Brookborough' offers piles of small yellow flowers while 'Yellow River' stands tall with buckets of big blooms. Ozark sundrops (*O. missouriensis*) has yellow flowers as big as your hand but demands excellent drainage like that found in rock gardens. To further confuse the name game among *Oenothera* species there is another species that thrives from Zone 7 into the tropics. The flowers of *O. drummondii* are yellow, but its common name is beach evening primrose.

  Zones 4–9

Lady Fern
(Athyrium filix-femina)

Damp shade has no better companion than lady fern, which is probably the first garden fern most people ever see. This is an elegant, well-behaved plant that can be counted on for years of brilliant green color. Tougher than she looks, the spring green fronds start each year as adorable new stems or croziers that may have red or pink hues. Soon they unfurl, tall, erect, and yes, fern green with a definite airy élan that lights up the darkest corners and lasts all season. No other fern has as many variations as this lady and many are named. Crested, crisscross designs and fancy plumes mark them, and one with both has a tongue-twisting name, 'Plumosum Cristatum'. 'Frizelliae' is a sweet dwarf fern with all the elegance of the much larger ladies. Finely cut leaves create a feathery, plume effect in 'Rotstiel' in fronds that can be 4 feet tall. In the same family, Japanese painted fern (*A. nipponicum* var. 'Pictum') has fronds in several shades of green from dark with gray tones to silver, blue-greens. Left alone, it spreads with endless color combinations in shade or morning sun. The surprising offspring of lady fern and this painted fern is 'Ghost', grown and loved for its spooky gray-green fronds.

  Zones 4–8 (marginal to Zone 9)

Rosemary
(*Rosmarinus officinalis*)

For green shades that can be dark moss green, gray-green, and even lighter hues when mature, rosemary can garner attention even before you detect it by its aroma. Young plants and old growth are darkest, heat and bright sun brings out the gray tones, and new growth starts out at grass green. Then its magnificent woodsy aroma adds dimension to this colorful, usually upright plant's appeal. The species is rounded at ground level with branches that curve wide and up, toward a point about 4 feet above the center. Its leaves are fat needles that also point up from the branches, creating an uplift-ing, optimistic mood. Prostrate rosemary ('*Prostratus*') is smaller overall with an arching habit that allows it to stand alone or spill over walls in a brilliant green row. Let rosemary be the centerpiece of a well-drained knot garden or xeriscape bed to best enjoy its color palette. This herb can grow in part shade, but in full sun its flow-ers attract pollinators to its blue or white lipped tubes of nectar. Where it is not garden-hardy, rosemary can be grown for years in a container protected from freezing and/or propagated each summer to grow as a house-plant in winter.

Zones 8–9 (marginal to Zone 7)

Shield Fern
(*Polystichum* spp.)

You could grow an entire grotto of diverse-looking ferns and never leave this group, beloved for a range of green shades and hardy good looks in damp, shady spaces. Sword fern (*P. munitum*) stands tall with fronds more than 4 feet long that arch gracefully up and away. Native to the western US and well adapted nationwide, sword fern's side growth can be tough to remove, but the elbow grease required pays off with large stands in a few seasons. Not limited in its appeal, either, Christmas fern (*P. acrostichoides*) hails from the East and was once a commercial source of holiday greenery. Often described as leathery, its fronds are longer than wide and are a deep, dark forest green. Two of the soft shield ferns (*P. setiferum*) offer charming shapes and habits and more points on the green spectrum. One group has blue-green fronds so divided that they seem crocheted into lacy loops. Equally upright with rust-colored mid-ribs, the fronds of the Divisilobum group are simpler in design. The individual leaflets are so small they might be beads strung on army green string. Southern shield fern (*Dryopteris*) shares its name with these ferns. Florescent lime green fronds are 3 feet tall and perennial in the South and West.

Zones 4–9

Wake Robin
(*Trillium*)

When spring pokes the shade garden, wake robin comes along for the ride, popping up in its native woodland environments across the globe. Those who seek truly unusual, long-lived perennial plants with a strong sense of place really should seek out local favorite *Trillium* species and encourage their use in garden culture. You will be rewarded with pleasing shades of green in leaves that can carpet shade under trees while other plants are still sleeping. Each leaf is wide and roughly heart-shaped; three leaves top each stem in nature's most perfect triangle of color. Some are solid green, like the best known of the bunch, great white trillium (*T. grandiflorum*), and its selections including 'Flore Peno'. But others offer surprising mottled, streaked, or painted leaves such as wake robin (*T. cuneatum*) with distinctive light and dark markings. There are more than two dozen trilliums native to the United States, some with flowers held up like scepters and other hidden, nodding under the leaves. All thrive in moist, organic soils where they can be undisturbed, and each is called different names depending on where it grows. Do not harvest any wildflower in its native stands; instead, seek them out from reputable nurseries and plant swaps.

Zones 4–8 (marginal to Zone 9)

Candytuft
(*Iberis sempervirens*)

Every garden bed looks better with a neat edge, and a low-growing flowering perennial can keep it spiffy if it is well-behaved in habit. Candytuft is such a plant, with crispy bunches of small emerald green leaves and flowers in dress whites. They bloom for weeks in early spring with a modest show in autumn in many areas. Mounds of bright white flowers crowd the leaves out of view, each one decked out in layers of crisp petals around greenish white eyes. The lowest, widest tier shows candytuft's toothy, squared off petals that are its signature, clean white smile. Candytuft has a clean, sweet fragrance that smells as cool as the plants look. The hardy plants bask in sunny or partly sunny beds with well-drained soil.

Unlike other perennials, candytuft can also be grown as an annual and allowed to reseed in place or collected for planting the next season. This strategy avoids the crispy leaves that excess heat and humidity can bring, but the plants can also be cut back in summer. Candytuft will experience senescence or summer dormancy in Zones 8b and 9; they return with cool weather and bloom intermittently all winter.

Zones 4–9

Eulalia Grass
(*Miscanthus*)

Other colors may flash and fade as summer wears on, but these ornamental grasses gain steam with the heat. Some say they best display their true colors, creams and whites, in autumn and winter but eulalia grass brings color all year. Spring sees them as heaps of long, thin blades piled up like haystacks; both solid greens and variegated leaves turn lustrous buff in fall. White and silvery hues take perennial style and grace to new levels: 'Variegatus' sets its standard with wide leaves and a stalwart form. 'Cabaret' is more upright, while 'Morning Light' has the thinnest leaves and the finest texture of all. But white and cream take center stage when eulalia grasses bloom with tall, fluffy plumes. Some of the best include 'Malepartus', with airy, soft-looking, creamy white plumes and 'Silver Feather', whose name nails the flowers' brilliant good looks. Eulalia grasses can be outstanding as focal point individuals or grown together into nearly impenetrable barriers to mark a property's edge. By the time in late fall or winter that you cut them down, the entire plants have donned wheat straw cloaks. Versatile and durable, eulalia grasses thrive in sun or part shade and any well-drained soil.

Zones 5–9

Great Globe Thistle
(*Echinops sphaerocephalus*)

If gardeners chose plants based on a menu of landscape attributes, this perennial might check off every item but its color tops the list. Great globe thistle defies comparison for its whites, which rock your expectations with gray, green, and even cream tones, depending on the day and the sunlight. Diversity reigns in perennial border design where plant height, texture, flower shape, and bloom season matter greatly. Great globe thistle has it all in a gorgeously bizarre plant, beginning with its rugged spiny leaves that are shaped like their relatives, artichokes and pasture thistles. Their undersides are cottony white and spaced wide along tall (4 to 6 feet) flower stems, affording you a great view of even more color. The plant's stems are oddly white, a rarity in perennial plants, and stiff in comparison to everything but tree branches. And then there are the flowers, the globes that are intricate round clusters that, more than anything else, resemble the Death Star in the movie *Star Wars*. Each tiny, sage-green bud stands like a map tack on the globe and opens into an elegant, feathery white, glowing orb. Great globe thistle would be a gawky mess, easily overlooked, were it not for its unexpected and unworldly whites.

Zones 4–9

Knotweed

(Persicaria polymorpha)

Like people, plants sometimes get a bad reputation from their relatives, and such is the case with knotweed. Aggressive and not especially pretty to most eyes, other *Persicaria* species and many related plants in the Polygonaceae family are mostly considered weeds. But even in the most dysfunctional families, there are exceptions—well behaved and lovely, perhaps forced to take another name to avoid recognition. This particular knotweed has become known as giant fleece flower, certainly a more descriptive, stylish name. The creamy white flowers are chic; upright clusters filled with knotty small blooms in profusion, their effect is rather like fistfuls of freshly sheared fleece. Even the flower buds are elegant, densely packed and light green atop stems 3 to 5 feet tall and thick with leaves shaped and colored like spireas. The muscular clumps can stand tall behind black-eyed Susans and other bold summer colors or contrast nicely with the cone-shaped blooms of purple butterfly bushes. They thrive in full sun with well-drained soil, tolerate some drought, and any amount of heat and humidity the climate offers. Call it knotweed or giant fleece flower, this perennial will be at home in cottage gardens and add crisp flair to naturalized garden designs.

Zones 4–9

Shasta Daisy

(Leucanthemum × superbum)

A bouquet sends a message: pansies are for thought, roses express emotions, and daisies—yellow centers with white ray petals flying in perfect circles—speak brightly in a welcome hello to friends. Leaves are John Deere-green and glossy, just the perfect supporting cast for the chaste white flower petals that surround a dense yellow disc center. Ironically, the story of this classic white flower comes shrouded in mystery, unlike its simple beauty. Whether you think Luther Burbank bred it from international stock or simply selected 'Shasta', he named it in 1901 after years of seeking its perfect white color and universally pleasing form. Many more bright whites have followed with single, double, frilly double, and curious anemone flower shapes, but a few stand out from the pack. 'Becky' follows true Shastas with later bloom and equally simple flowers on a more forgiving plant, but all these daisies do best in moderate environments without extremes of wet and dry soils. 'Esther Read' has delightful fully double flowers on a 2-foot plant, while 'Aglaia' loosens up its doubled petals for an occasional glimpse at its yellow center. 'Alaska' is grown from seed yet displays great uniformity in both plants and crisp, white, single flowers.

Zones 5–8

Groundcovers

H. micrantha 'Palace Purple'

H. sanguinea

Coral Bells

(*Heuchera*)

Sometimes you think you know a plant, and then everything changes, like the day your teenager gets her driver's license. Coral bells (*H. sanguinea*) used to be a nice, predictable groundcover with ruffled green leaves and cute pink flowers. But late in the last century a plethora of quite different selections and new releases from breeders appeared in landscapes and garden centers. Leaf colors from practically pink to purple, orange, yellow, and rainbows of mixed shades now decorate sunny sites in the North and partial shade in the South. The world of coral bells has changed so dramatically that many gardeners do not recognize the original and know only *Heuchera* as the name for these fabulous plants. They are still polite mounds about a foot tall and wide, have fancy leaves in a dense clump, and belong in every well-drained garden soil nationwide. Their versatility makes the garden possibilities almost unlimited. Coral bells can fill a bed, edge a sidewalk, or take their place in the front row of a perennial border. The incredible array of color patterns enables you to lay out a mixed-up crazy quilt or reinforce your theme palette. Round-leafed coral bells suit a casual design as when they are used to soften the hard lines of a deck. Deeply cut edges or crazy outlines almost like maple leaves make a stronger statement of order and formality. Groups of three plants repeated along a curved bed can bring comforting unity and stability.

- 'Alabama Sunrise' has yellow-green leaves that feature bright red veins in spring and summer. They are deeply lobed, wrinkled, and mesmerizing.
- 'Amber Waves' undulates with shades of gold and apricot on scalloped leaves that might be piles of fancy oak leaves but for their pale pink flowers.
- Deep purple leaves with white edges emphasize the extravagant ruffles that distinguish 'Amethyst Myst'.
- A calico tapestry of orange, red, and yellow hues mark 'Peach Crisp'. Its leaves are both lobed and ruffled for superior colorful dimension.
- 'Southern Comfort' has rounder leaves that seem to roll out of their crown in shades of light orange and apricot.
- 'Delta Dawn' has leaves that are veined, lobed, and edged. Dark orange-red veins create intricate patterns on peachy backgrounds with gold-green rims and flower stems.
- 'Rave On' gets attention for shiny silver leaves with red underneath and tall spikes crowded with tiny coral flowers. Whoever named it can be forgiven for the effusive name—this plant earns it.

Groundcover choices use color and growth habit to establish the basis of a top-down design. A flat, dark green profile emphasizes everything above and around it while a mat of looser, lighter green offers contrast to other plants in the design.

Athyrium niponicum var. pictum

Dryopteris marginalis

Hardy Ferns

This group refers to evergreen and deciduous ferns with average clumps 2 feet by 2 feet or smaller. In practical terms, hardy ferns may be ankle-, calf-, or almost knee-high, but their clumps must grow dense to be considered a groundcover. They are well suited for living mulches and low profile beds as well as in cameo roles in the perennial border or shady grotto. Hardy ferns offer a boatload of plants to choose from that diverge wildly in characteristic color and texture. There are selections for every zone, shade density, and green hue you desire, in textures from boldly coarse to frilly fine. Brilliant examples of the group include wood ferns (*Dryopteris*) and cliff ferns (*Woodsia*).

Wood ferns (Zones 5 through 8) include crested buckler (*D. dilitata* 'Cristata'), which ups the ante on exuberant, girly good looks with crested tips on each shiny frond. Male wood fern (*D. filiz-mas*) is native to the United States and has big clumps of emerald green fronds that are evergreen in warm winter areas. Champion's wood fern (*D. championii*) has Christmas green fronds and light lime green new growth. It is 2 feet tall and wider, with arching, yard-long fronds. With similar dimensions, Formosa wood fern (*D. formosana*) has fronds that are lighter in color and texture with especially wide bases. Hardier still, fragrant woodfern

(*D. fragrans*) thrives in moist environments yet can tolerate some drought without damage in northern zones.

Cliff ferns (Zones 5 through 8) hail from around the globe, including all US states and are usually 6 inches tall or measured falling over rocks as their name implies. Tolerant of sunnier sites than most ferns, they include the grass-green blunt-lobed woodsia (*W. obtusa*) a loose, airy fern with tufts of stems about 10 inches tall in the garden. Oblong or rusty woodsia (*W. ilvensis*) is tougher than it looks. Open and upright in form, the ribbon-green fronds are almost lacy.

Hardy in Zones 4 through 9, **Japanese painted fern** (*Athyrium niponicum* var. *pictum*) defies imagination with its exotic, enchanting beauty. Its fronds are lacy, light and dark green with a cloak of silver and claret that is most unexpected. A patch among muscular hosta and ginger plants delivers stunning textural contrast in brilliant color. In Zones 5 through 8, other *Athyrium* cultivars with surprising color include 'Branford Beauty' with burgundy stems and silvery fronds and 'Lady in Red' noted for scarlet red stems. 'Silver Falls' radiates in morning sun with reddish pink stems and purplish leaf veins.

Bearberry
(Arctostaphylos uva-ursi)

If you could stand up a single stem of bearberry, it might be taller than you are—but this groundcover's habit never lets on. Its profile is not over a foot high yet the rough red stems can spread 6 feet, twisting around and growing together into delightfully dense clumps. The leaves are glossy, round at the outer edge, slightly spoon-shaped, and evergreen in shades from lime to forest green. The flowers are pinkish white, bell-shaped, and a sweet surprise as their fragrance wafts up to your nose in late spring. Soon the power punch of color arrives in crimson red berries with such sheen they might have been polished. If bearberry were a woman, you'd say she is the girl-next-door—cute, clean, and polished. A modern selection of this storied plant, 'Massachusetts' is especially showy with great garden potential. Smaller and with a thicker, more compact form than the native, its flowers and berries are a bit larger, too. Native from Alaska to Virginia (and Greenland), the plants thrive in poor, acid soils and so make an especially colorful statement in difficult garden areas. Let the runners roam to show off their true prostrate habit and create a colorful view where few plants could.

Zones 4–6 (marginal to Zone 7)

Bunchberry
(Cornus canadensis)

Although its name may not seem inspired, bunchberry (also called creeping dogwood) describes this groundcover quite well. It has shiny, cardinal-red berries in, well, bunches, atop crisp, five-leaf clusters that turn glorious fall shades of red and purple. Look closely and you'll see the resemblance to its relatives, the dogwood trees. The leaves are broadly oval, slightly curved around the edges with a pointed tip. They seem longer than they are because each leaf has distinctive veins running its length, and their color ranges from crayon-green to hues with yellow tinges. Growing at a moderate pace in well-drained soils, bunchberry spreads with underground rhizomes to form thick drifts in shady beds. Late spring brings the flowers, tight little clusters that would be nondescript but for the four satiny bracts around them. More understated than those on the trees, creeping dogwood's flowers do shine unlike any other groundcover in late spring. The bright berries form in summer and persist unless eaten by wildlife until the first cool snap. Then the leaves take the stage for weeks with striking red hues from candy apple to almost purple. Bunchberry fits neatly under trees and peeks out from the edges of shrubs and makes a perfect living mulch at no more than 6 inches tall.

Zones 4–7 (marginal to Zone 8)

Cinquefoil

(*Potentilla*)

Cinquefoil quite literally takes its name from the fourteenth-century term for "five leaf" and is not named for its petals. But their perfect symmetry has timeless appeal. The plants will surge and spill, sending leafy branches every which way to set up for a long bloom season of flashy red flowers. There are five petals in each, surrounding a bright yellow center; in garden varieties, each flower can be as wide as the saucer for a teacup. 'Red Ace' ages its flowers from red to apricot and sometimes several shades appear at once. 'Red Robin' is flirty with pale yellow tones on the underside of scarlet red petals. Cinquefoil plants are not tiny, creeping groundcovers meant to edge a neat bed. The plants average 18 to 24 inches tall and spread into dense mats that are much wider and so can best be considered in this group for this pleasing habit. Palmate, or hand-shaped, leaves grow into thick bunches of tiny fingers reaching up and out in shades of grayish green. The plants thrive in moist, well-drained soil and full sun, but the flowers will last longer and hold their colors with afternoon shade. Their versatility earns space in designs from quaint cottage style to clean, modern, low-maintenance plans.

Zones 4–7

Stonecrop

(*Sedum*)

Without question, stonecrops solve lots of design dilemmas with serene, chic style. The plants and flowers are undemanding, and their colors are bright and cheery, especially the reds and pinks. Well-drained and poor soils welcome this groundcover that roots everywhere a stem or shiny leaf makes contact. They rapidly spread wider than tall across open space, gravel, and gentle slopes but are well behaved and easily kept in their place. Tiny Lydian stonecrop (*S. lydium*) has clusters of tightly wrapped leaves, green cylinders with red frosting just lighter than the red stems. 'Ruby Glow' (*S. middendorfianum*), at 10 inches tall, looks like its name, with starry flowers in shades from rose to ruby to garnet. Even its leaves have a dark red-purple sheen. Two-row sedums (*S. spurium*) bring brilliant pinks and reds to plants 3 to 6 inches tall, depending on variety. 'Dragon's Blood' shimmers with rose pink hues in flowers and darker leaves. Diminutive 'John Creech' is but 2 inches tall yet covered in bright pink flowers from summer to fall. A variegated two-row sedum adds pink stripes to its green and white leaves for added dimension in its dense mat. Almost a foot high, 'Vera Jameson' rounds out this group with pink flowers in the mauve range.

Zones 4–9

Brass Buttons

(*Leptinella* 'Platt's Black')

If your design sense says there should be a ferny-looking plant for sunny sites, brass buttons, particularly 'Platt's Black', will suit your style. This purple is so dark that its moniker truly suits; the leaves are nearly black and oil-slick shiny. They are 2 inches long, almost an inch wide, and taper slightly down like a fern frond. Each leaf has tiny, flat leaflets all along its length to form mats of purple and purplish green that are no more than a few inches tall, but healthy rhizomes will spread much wider. Well-drained, organic and preferably acidic soils provide optimum growing conditions for brass buttons. The habit and leaf detail of 'Platt's Black' resemble button fern (*Nephrolepsis*) if it were camouflaged with deep purple spray paint. This New Zealand native is rugged enough that you can walk gently on established plantings without damaging them and even mow the flowers off to increase leafy growth. Its gold flowers and small berries are not very showy but do add contrasting texture to the leaves in summer. Brass buttons is a full-sun plant everywhere except Zones 8b and 9 where partly shady sites will best maintain the leaf color of 'Platt's Black'.

Zones 4–8

Carpet Bugle

(*Ajuga reptans*)

Sweet rosettes of leaves that range from dark green to purple look impossibly quirky, their veins so tight that they seem stitched into waffle patterns. Each leaf is slightly scalloped and flares to a round outer edge for even more ground-hugging interest. They are gathered into a ground-hugging crown that spreads in sun or shade and wears its spring flowers like a tiara made of cloisonné blue beads. Because they are packed so tightly onto the flower stem, each horn is squished so its lower lobe sticks out like a trumpeter's pouty lip. Also known as bugleweed, this groundcover has gone uptown in recent decades with a plethora of stunning selections. 'Black Scallop' looks unworldly with deep purple leaves that glisten in sunlight even on a dry day. 'Mahogany' has leaves that are redder and rounder on a slightly shorter plant. 'Burgundy Glow' has purple new growth amid leaves that age to blue green with white markings. 'Dixie Chip' shows different variegation, green, off-white, and red-purple leaves and deep violet flowers. 'Chocolate Chip' has lighter, Delft-blue flowers, and 'Atropurpurea' even has purple stems. Especially small 'Purple Brocade' has shorter bloom stems in tight, purple-blue clusters.

Zones 4–9

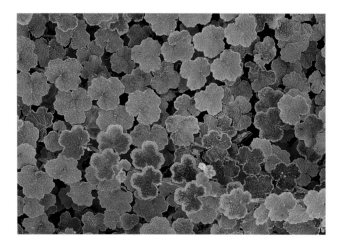

Creeping Raspberry
(*Rubus pentalobus*)

Also known as creeping bramble and ornamental bramble, this is an evergreen groundcover that is virtually indestructible. It is favored for four-season interest and lives up to its billing with dark purple-red and sometimes bronze fall color that lasts until spring when the clumps turn green with new growth. Their shades are rich like the hues woven into quality tapestries that depict knights and derring-do. The leaves are puckered into lumpy, round heart shapes, some lobed and/or slightly wavy on their edges. They pack visual muscle and are held stiffly on strong, short stems that deliver three-dimensional interest, unusual in such a low-growing plant. Creeping raspberry is at home in full sun and partial shade, in almost any soil that drains well. It needs only minimal amounts of water once established and will crawl and sometimes run in every direction from its crown to form a dense mat 2 to 4 inches tall. White flowers keep spring interesting, followed by raspberry-like fruits that can be purple, red, or golden yellow for more color well into summer. Creeping raspberry is at home in beds and borders but also in large containers and rock gardens where it can spill over surfaces with panache.

Zones 6–9

Lungwort
(*Pulmonaria*)

Shady places need color to brighten them, never more so than in early spring when everyone is looking for signs of the new season. Lungworts have it—green, silver, and mottled leaves put on flowers in purple and blue shades to warm your heart and the garden scene. The blooms come in clusters that emerge from dark, red-purple buds that pop open into blue, purple, or pink bell shapes. Long leaves range from a few inches to more than a foot long from the clump to their tip and taper sweetly to form bubbly mounds. The plants spread by rhizomes, but slowly, and some also reseed to further build their numbers. They do best in rich soil that stays just moist but also drains away the excess, yet can adapt to slightly less ideal conditions. Long-leaved lungwort (*P. longifolia*) dazzles with pure blue flowers, and its selection 'Cevennensis' is noted for leaves 18 to 20 inches long. Bethlehem sage (*P. saccharata*) has wild silver leaf markings, especially prominent in 'Milky Way', with dark blue blooms. A fabulous hybrid, 'Roy Davidson' has precious pale blue flowers atop long, spotted leaves. 'Silver Bouquet' features shiny silver leaves and incredible blue and pink blossoms.

Zones 4–8

Fairy Wings

(*Epimedium*)

Fairy wings, also known as bishop's hat and less romantically called barrenwort, invites close inspection. They seldom look as tall as their 1-foot height and spread slowly into piles of little leaves shaped like organic valentines. They offer plenty of pizazz all by themselves, especially those colored in shades of bronze, gold, and red. Each is deeply notched at the stem end and held aloft on a thin, stiff stem. The result is a slightly flattened clump with a neat profile in the garden. Then the yellow flowers appear, tiny individuals arranged in loose bunches that fill the space in early spring sometimes before the leaves. They may be pastel shades or much brighter, like *E. warleyense* with flowers that are bright orange and yellow. Long-spurred fairy wings (*E. grandiflorum*) is 8 inches tall, a bit wider, and has quirky, spiky leaves. Two more barrenworts are slightly less hardy than the others They are, however, better suited to Zone 8b and sometimes Zone 9, where they are reliably evergreen. *E. × perralchicum* can be more than a foot tall with twice the spread and its selection, 'Frohnleiten' brings flowers an inch wide in mounds to the spring garden. Of similar size, *E. perralderianum* adds brown spurs in contrast to its sunny yellow flowers.

Zones 4–9

Moneywort

(*Lysimachia nummularia* 'Aurea')

Golden yellow heading toward chartreuse in shade, moneywort, or creeping Jenny, spreads its cloak of round leaves quickly. Each leaf is the size of a quarter or a dime, and they are stacked in whorls around short, equally colorful stems. They run across bare ground, rooting anywhere a stem hits the soil, and spill out of containers like the ruffles on a goofy teenager's tuxedo shirt. This shade, bright and compelling, defines happy yellow in plants made for moist, sunny sites and makes an indelible imprint on all who see it. The yellow leaves are thick in dimension and in growth pattern with a relentless positive attitude—they never flinch in thunderstorms and can tolerate brief dry spells without losing leaves or color. About 4 inches tall, creeping Jenny's profile is upright yet gently undulating, upbeat and almost fluffy. Moneywort, another common name for this plant, is taken from the traditional term for weed, "wort," referring to its gold coin-shaped leaves and flowers. Creeping jenny is a seventeenth-century term for whooping cough, and the plant was used in its treatment. Equally popular, 'Golden Globes' is a green-leaved relative (*L. procumbens*) with charming yellow flowers surrounding a red center.

Zones 4–9

Yellow Archangel

(*Lamium galeobdolon*)

For a plant that is otherwise known as dead nettle, *Lamium* has much to offer in the color garden. Deep shade presents challenges to seasonal yellow color beyond a few plants that do not lose their hues there, mostly in their leaves such as hostas. Yellow archangel meets this need with distinctive flowers in mellow yellow shades that are quaintly charming. Most of its flower parts seem to peek shyly from under one big petal above them, an exaggerated cap. Their effect is clever, as if it had been drawn to attract attention from visitors to the difficult areas under trees and between them. Shallow-rooted and ready to spread on stems that creep at ground level, the plants are quite drought tolerant once established. Yellow archangel might also be exalted (as its name suggests) for its striking silver and gray leaves painted to exaggerate their elongated heart shapes. The plants establish themselves with steady vigor, spreading both above- and belowground by stolons and rhizomes. The clumps are a foot tall with flowering stems held several inches above that to create a round mound with leafy antennas flush with yellow blooms. 'Hermann's Pride' has slightly narrower, toothy leaves and lemon yellow flowers with a sweet, sophisticated air.

Zones 4–9

Lily Turf

(*Liriope spicata*)

Sometimes a plant seems to be everywhere, and we are tempted to deem it too common to grow. But there's a reason for its popularity, and in the case of lily turf, that reason is the color green. Dark and rich, the strappy leaves are as green as the finest pool table felt and just as lustrous. The entire plant is no more than a foot tall, yet there are scores of leaves springing from each clump. They form a mound that is neat but never boring because just enough of the leaves stand up at attention—and gain yours. Muscular spikes of purple-blue flowers join them in summer and are followed by round, black berries.

'Big Blue' lives up to its name with thick spikes of blue flowers that seem to punch their way out of the clump in summer. Any well-drained soil can support lily turf; with regular watering and annual fertilizing in spring, it will show its vibrant colors for years. Lily turf plants are best maintained by cutting off the old leaves in late winter before the new ones arise in the center of the plant. Divide clumps every three years for more flowers and the neatest looks.

Zones 5–9

Pachysandra

(*Pachysandra terminalis*)

Evergreen groundcovers are a treasure when their colors sparkle and mark the seasons with subtle changes. Pachysandra is also called spurge, although that is the name of a group of lawn weeds and hardly suits this beautiful, ground-hugging plant. Adaptable to all but the driest sites, its colors respond to the available sun, with the darkest bottle greens in deep shade and yellow-green, almost chartreuse hues in sun. In high shade, pachysandra's shiny evergreen leaves gleam like emerald green gems that would make a jeweler proud. The leaves are 2 inches long, slightly toothed, and arranged in flat clusters called whorls to create a dynamic planting that refracts every ray of sun. Its stems are also green, with the delightful habit of rooting where they touch the ground, ensuring thick stands for years. In spring, flowers that are small white brushes add interest to passersby and are another reason to grow pachysandra along walkways and under trees near the house. Sometimes called Japanese spurge, it's not to be confused with Allegheny spurge, a native *Pachysandra* (*P. procumbens*) with a coarser habit and ability to live in deeper shade and wetter conditions. Its green is deeper, too, with blue-gray overtones.

Zones 4–9

Bishop's Weed

(*Aegopodium podagraria* 'Variegatum')

Green leaves with white variegation grab whatever light reaches shady gardens and bounces it around, illuminating the space. Their presence adds interest, dimension, and texture to the view, and also continuity with their constant color. Not all plants have strong variegation, neatly defined in each leaf, and not all hold their white variegation all year. Even in shade, bishop's weed fulfills this mission; in brighter beds it can be a guiding white beacon along paths and in between shrubs. Not every leaf is painted alike, and each of three leaflets can vary greatly within one leaf cluster. A bit rounded in the middle and a little toothy around the edges, the leaves have green feathery patterns drawn with white rims. Sometimes white or green consumes most of the leaf, but usually it's a fascinating mixed bag of patterns. A foot tall and half again as wide, bishop's weed quickly grows into a thick mat of color in almost any soil that drains well. The flowers are a minor feature and can be sheared off to prevent seedlings that may lack strong coloration. If any shoots are ever entirely green, they should be removed, too, so the striking green and white can dominate.

Zones 4–9

Dwarf Fountain Grass
(*Pennisetum alopecuroides*)

If you are in the camp that feels names like "Little Bunny" are too cute by half, call it "groundcover fountain grass" and grow it anyway. Few others even come close to this little ornamental grass for color and cover at ground level. No more than 18 inches tall and a bit wider, this grass forms a dense mat of fine-textured green leaves that goes creamy ecru in late summer or fall, depending on the zone. Its puffy white flowers appear in late spring atop thin, wiry stems. Each bloom is shaped like a capsule and comprised of dozens of tiny florets and nods with a little wink in the breeze. They are decidedly cute, some have a slight cockeyed bend to the inflorescence, and they are fuzzy in a silly, attractive way. Slightly larger 'Hameln' has longer, narrower flowers, creamy tan spires on an equally compact plant. In between the other two in height and plume shape is 'Piglet'. Dwarf fountain grasses are best grown in full sun in northern zones but with afternoon shade farther south. The need for well-drained soil and regular watering make these grasses good companions for many flowering perennials.

Zone 5–9

Lamb's Ear
(*Stachys byzantina*)

The first glimpse of this perennial in a garden bed or planter can be cause for a double take as you look back to confirm the view. Fuzzy, oddly white leaves demand closer observation, which reveals a thick white coating of baby-fine hairs soft as eiderdown all over them. The "hairs" are white in full or part sun, glisten when morning dew sits on them, and shine like silver when the light is just right at dusk. Each elongated oval leaf is wide in the middle and gently pointed at the end; someone saw a resemblance to lamb's ear and named it. Natural whimsy and tactile joy can be overlooked if a plant's colors are not as magnetic as these whites are, but lamb's ear goes further. As a featured player along the edge of a perennial planting, its color reflects well, literally and figuratively. Lamb's ear plants stay close to the ground and spread rapidly into a dense clump. Where necessary, control their rampant nature by removing young sprouts promptly and removing flowers before they set seed. Two selections never bloom: 'Silver Carpet' and big lamb's ears, 'Helen von Stein'. The latter is a larger plant, still under a foot tall and twice as wide.

Zones 4–9

USDA Hardiness Zone Map

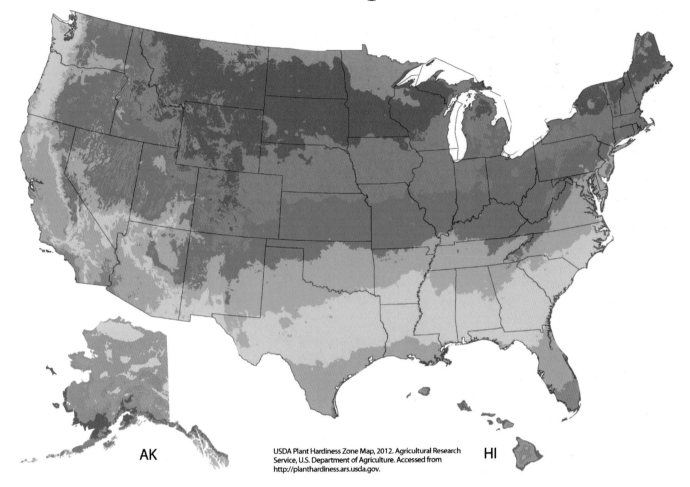

AK

HI

USDA Plant Hardiness Zone Map, 2012. Agricultural Research Service, U.S. Department of Agriculture. Accessed from http://planthardiness.ars.usda.gov.

Average Annual Extreme Minimum Temperature
1976–2005

Temp (F)	Zone	Temp (C)	Temp (F)	Zone	Temp (C)
-60 to -55	1a	-51.1 to -48.3	5 to 10	7b	-15 to -12.2
-55 to -50	1b	-48.3 to -45.6	10 to 15	8a	-12.2 to -9.4
-50 to -45	2a	-45.6 to -42.8	15 to 20	8b	-9.4 to -6.7
-45 to -40	2b	-42.8 to -40	20 to 25	9a	-6.7 to -3.9
-40 to -35	3a	-40 to -37.2	25 to 30	9b	-3.9 to -1.1
-35 to -30	3b	-37.2 to -34.4	30 to 35	10a	-1.1 to 1.7
-30 to -25	4a	-34.4 to -31.7	35 to 40	10b	1.7 to 4.4
-25 to -20	4b	-31.7 to -28.9	40 to 45	11a	4.4 to 7.2
-20 to -15	5a	-28.9 to -26.1	45 to 50	11b	7.2 to 10
-15 to -10	5b	-26.1 to -23.3	50 to 55	12a	10 to 12.8
-10 to -5	6a	-23.3 to -20.6	55 to 60	12b	12.8 to 15.6
-5 to 0	6b	-20.6 to -17.8	60 to 65	13a	15.6 to 18.3
0 to 5	7a	-17.8 to -15	65 to 70	13b	18.3 to 21.1

Planting Chart

GENUS	COMMON NAME	ORIGINS	GARDEN SOIL TYPE	EXPOSURE
TREES				
Acer	maple	US/Japan	richly organic	sun/sun to part shade
Aesculus	buckeye	US woodlands	well-drained, organic	part sun to part shade
Amelanchier	downy serviceberry	US woods' edge	richly organic	sun to part shade
Arbutus	strawberry tree	Europe west	richly organic	sun to part shade
Asimina	pawpaw	US east and central	well-drained, organic	sun to shade
Betula	river birch	US	well-drained, organic	sun
Catalpa	catalpa	US south	adaptable	sun
Cercis	redbud	US east to Mexico	adaptable	sun to part shade
Chilopsis	desert willow	US southwest	well-drained	sun to part sun
Clerodendrum	glorybower	China and Japan	well-drained, organic	sun to part shade
Cornus	flowering dogwood	US east to Mexico	well-drained, organic	part sun to part shade
Cotinus	smoketree	US/Europe to China	well-drained	sun to part sun
Ginkgo	ginkgo	China	adaptable	sun
Hibiscus	rose of Sharon	China, India	well-drained, organic	sun
Juniperus	redcedar	US east and central	adaptable	sun
Kalopanax	castor-aralia	Asia from Russia to Korea	well-drained, organic	sun to part shade
Koelreuteria	golden raintree	Korean, China, Japan	richly organic	sun
Laburnum	golden chaintree	Europe central	well-drained, organic	sun
Lagerstroemia	crape myrtle	China, Korea	adaptable	sun
Ligustrum	Japanese privet	Japan, Korea	adaptable	sun to part shade
Liquidambar	sweetgum	US east to Mexico	adaptable	sun
Liriodendron	tulip poplar	US east and south	well-drained, organic	sun
Magnolia	flowering magnolia	hybrids/Japan	well-drained, organic	sun to part sun
Malus	flowering crabapple	hybrids	well-drained, organic	sun
Metasequoia	dawn redwood	China	adaptable	sun
Nyssa	blackgum	US, Canada	well-drained, organic	sun
Ostrya	American hophornbeam	US, Canada	well-drained, organic	sun
Paulownia	empress tree	China	adaptable	sun
Pinus	pine	Europe/Japan/US	well-drained	sun
Pistacia	Chinese pistasche	China, Taiwan, Philippines	adaptable	sun
Platanus	American sycamore	US	richly organic	sun
Populus	quaking aspen	US, Canada	adaptable	sun to part sun
Prunus	ornamental cherry, plum	Asia	well-drained, organic	sun to part sun
Quercus	oak	US	adaptable	sun to part sun
Salix	weeping willow	Asia	richly organic	sun
Sassafras	sassafras	US east and south	richly organic, acid	part sun to part shade
Stewartia	stewartia	Korea, Japan	richly organic	part sun to part shade
Taxodium	bald cypress	US east and south	adaptable	sun
Tilia	pendant silver linden	SW Asia	well-drained, organic	sun
Ulmus	elm	US, Canada	adaptable	sun
Viburnum	blackhaw	US east and south	adaptable	part sun to part shade
Vitex	chastetree	Europe, Asia	adaptable	sun
Zelkova	zelkova	Japan	adaptable	sun to part sun

WATER	FERTILIZER	PRUNING
regularly	tree formula spring, summer	only to remove dead wood
regularly in summer	tree formula early spring	while young to shape
regularly	tree formula early spring	only to remove dead wood
regularly	tree formula in spring	only to remove dead wood
regularly in summer	tree formula spring, summer	only to remove dead wood
regularly	tree formula early spring	to keep sprouts clipped off
regularly in summer	tree formula early spring	while young to shape
regularly	flowering tree formula summer	only to remove dead wood
grow on dry side	flowering tree formula summer	cut back dead wood in spring
regularly	flowering tree formula spring	while young to shape
regularly in summer	flowering tree formula summer	only to remove dead wood
grow on dry side	flowering tree formula summer	while young to shape
grow on dry side	tree formula spring, summer	while young to shape
regularly	flowering tree formula spring, summer	cut back dead wood in spring
grow on dry side	tree formula early spring	shear into shape in winter
regularly in summer	tree formula spring, summer	clip off spent flowers
regularly in summer	flowering tree formula summer	select 1 or 3 trunks
regularly	flowering tree formula spring, summer	shape after flowering
regularly	flowering tree formula spring, summer	keep sprouts clipped off
grow on dry side	tree formula spring and summer	shape after flowering
grow on dry side	tree formula summer	while young to shape
grow on dry side	tree formula summer	while young to shape
regularly in summer	flowering tree formula summer	only to remove dead wood
regularly in summer	flowering tree formula summer	only to remove dead wood
grow on dry side	tree formula spring	shear into shape in winter
regularly	tree formula spring	while young to shape
grow on dry side	tree formula spring	only to remove dead wood
regularly	flowering tree formula summer	while young to shape
grow on dry side	tree formula spring	only to remove dead wood
regularly in summer	tree formula spring	only to remove dead wood
regularly	tree formula spring	only to remove dead wood
regularly in summer	tree formula spring	while young to shape
regularly	flowering tree formula summer	cherry: tip prune in winter
regularly in summer	tree formula spring	while young to shape
regularly	tree formula spring, summer	trim to keep branches off ground
regularly	tree formula spring	only to remove dead wood
regularly in summer	flowering tree formula spring	only to remove dead wood
regularly in summer	tree formula spring	while young to shape
regularly in summer	tree formula spring	while young to shape
regularly in summer	tree formula spring	only to remove dead wood
regularly	flowering tree formula spring, summer	to shape after flowering
regularly	flowering tree formula spring	cut back dead wood in spring
regularly in summer	tree formula spring	while young to shape

GENUS	COMMON NAME	ORIGINS	GARDEN SOIL TYPE	EXPOSURE
SHRUBS				
Abelia	glossy abelia	China	richly organic	sun to part shade
Berberis	barberry	Japan	well-drained, organic	sun to part shade
Callicarpa	beautyberry	US, Japan	richly organic	part sun to part shade
Calycanthus	sweetshrub	US south	well-drained, organic	part sun
Camellia	sasanqua	Asia	richly organic	part sun to part shade
Ceanothus	ceanothus	US, Mexico	well-drained, organic	sun to part shade
Chaenomeles	flowering quince	China	well-drained, organic	sun to part shade
Clethra	summersweet	US east and south	well-drained, organic	part sun to part shade
Corylus	purple filbert	Europe	adaptable	sun
Cotoneaster	cotoneaster	China	well-drained	sun
Daphne	daphne	China	well-drained, organic	shade
Deutzia	deutzia	Japan	richly organic	part sun to part shade
Euonymus	euonymus	Japan	well-drained	sun to part shade
Exochorda	pearlbush	China	adaptable	sun to part shade
Fatsia	fatsia	Japan	richly organic	part shade to shade
Forsythia	forsythia	China	well-drained, organic	sun to part shade
Fothergilla	fothergilla	US	richly organic	part sun to part shade
Genista	Dyer's greenwood	Europe, Asia	well-drained	sun
Hydrangea	hydrangea	US east	richly organic	part sun to shade
Ilex	holly	China, Korea	well-drained, organic	sun to part sun
Kalmia	mountain laurel	Canada, US	well-drained, acid	part sun to part shade
Kerria	kerria	China	richly organic	part shade
Loropetalum	loropetalum, fringe flower	China	well-drained, organic	sun to part sun
Mahonia	grape holly	Japan	richly organic	part shade to shade
Nandina	heavenly bamboo	China	adaptable	sun to shade
Photinia	Chinese photinia	China	adaptable	sun to part sun
Physocarpus	ninebark	Canada, US	adaptable	sun
Pieris	pieris	China, Myanmar	richly organic	part sun to part shade
Potentilla	cinquefoil	China	well-drained	sun
Rhododendron	native azalea	US east	richly organic	part sun to part shade
Rhus	fragrant sumac	US east	well-drained, organic	part sun to part shade
Rosa	rose	Asia	well-drained, organic	sun
Spiraea	spirea	Asia	well-drained, organic	sun to part shade
Syringa	lilac	China	well-drained, organic	sun
Viburnum	viburnum	US, Japan	well-drained, organic	part sun to part shade
Yucca	Adam's needle	US	well-drained, organic	sun to part shade
PERENNIALS				
Astilbe	astilbe	China and hybrids	richly organic	part shade to shade
Athyrium	lady fern	US east	richly organic	part shade to shade
Clematis	clematis	US, Japan, China	well-drained, organic	sun to part sun
Columbine	columbine	US	richly organic	part shade to shade
Coreopsis	tickseed	US	well-drained, organic	sun

WATER	FERTILIZER	PRUNING
regularly in summer	flowering shrub formula spring, summer	to shape after flowering
grow on dry side	shrub formula in spring, summer	to shape in spring
regularly in summer	shrub formula in spring	to shape in spring
regularly in summer	flowering shrub formula in spring	to shape after flowering
regularly in summer	flowering shrub formula in spring	to shape after flowering
grow on dry side	flowering shrub formula spring, summer	to shape after flowering
regularly in summer	flowering shrub formula spring	to shape after flowering
regularly	flowering shrub formula spring, summer	to shape after flowering
regularly in summer	shrub formula in spring, summer	to shape in spring
grow on dry side	shrub formula in spring	to shape in spring
regularly	flowering shrub formula spring, summer	seldom if ever
regularly in summer	flowering shrub formula spring	to shape after flowering
regularly in summer	shrub formula in spring	to shape in spring
regularly in summer	flowering shrub formula in spring	to shape after flowering
regularly	shrub formula in spring	only to remove dead wood
regularly in summer	flowering shrub formula in spring, summer	to shape after flowering
regularly in summer	flowering shrub formula in spring	to shape after flowering
grow on dry side	flowering shrub formula in spring	to shape after flowering
regularly	flowering shrub formula in spring, summer	to shape after flowering
regularly in summer	shrub formula in spring	to shape in spring
regularly in summer	flowering shrub formula in spring	to shape after flowering
regularly in summer	flowering shrub formula in spring, summer	to shape after flowering
regularly in summer	flowering shrub formula spring, summer	to shape after flowering
regularly in summer	flowering shrub formula spring, summer	to shape in spring
grow on dry side	shrub formula in spring	only to remove dead wood
grow on dry side	shrub formula in spring	to shape in spring
regularly in summer	shrub formula in spring	to shape in spring
regularly	shrub formula in spring	to shape in spring
grow on dry side	shrub formula in spring	to shape after flowering
regularly	flowering shrub formula spring	to shape after flowering
regularly	shrub formula in spring	cut back dead wood in spring
regularly	shrub or rose formula spring, summer	cut back late winter, early spring
regularly in summer	flowering shrub formula spring, summer	to shape in spring and after flowering
regularly in summer	flowering shrub formula in spring	to shape after flowering
regularly	shrub formula in spring	to shape after flowering
grow on dry side	shrub formula in spring	seldom if ever
regularly	flowering perennial formula in spring	remove spent flowers, cut back when dormant
regularly	fern or perennial formula	remove spend fronds
regularly in summer	flowering perennial formula in spring	remove spent flowers, cut back when dormant
regularly in summer	flowering perennial formula in spring	remove spent flower stalks
grow on dry side	flowering perennial formula in spring	allow to reseed

GENUS	COMMON NAME	ORIGINS	GARDEN SOIL TYPE	EXPOSURE
Dianthus	cottage pinks	Europe	well-drained, organic	sun to part shade
Echinacea	coneflower	US	well-drained, organic	sun to part shade
Echinops	great globe thistle	Europe	adaptable	sun to part sun
Eupatorium	Joe-pye weed	US	adaptable	sun to part sun
Gaillardia	blanket flower	US	well-drained	sun
Hemerocallis	daylily	Asia	well-drained, organic	sun
Hosta	hosta	Asia	richly organic	part sun to shade
Iberis	candytuft	Europe	well-drained, organic	sun to part shade
Iris	iris	US, Asia	well-drained	sun to part shade
Leucanthemum	daisy	Europe	well-drained	sun
Liatris	gayfeather	US	richly organic	sun to part shade
Lobelia	cardinal flower	US	richly organic	part sun to shade
Miscanthus	ornamental grasses	Asia	well-drained	sun to part shade
Oenothera	sundrops	Mexico	well-drained	sun
Paeonia	peony	US, Asia	richly organic	sun to part sun
Penstemon	beardtongue	US	well-drained, organic	sun to part sun
Persicaria	knotweed	US, Asia	well-drained	sun to part shade
Phlox	phlox	US	well-drained, organc	part sun to part shade
Polystichum	sword fern	Asia	richly organic	part shade to shade
Rosmarinus	rosemary	Europe	well-drained	sun to part shade
Rudbeckia	black-eyed Susan	US	well-drained, organic	sun
Salvia	sage	US, Mexico, Europe	well-drained, organic	sun to part shade
Stokesia	Stokes' aster	US	well-drained	sun to part shade
Trillium	wake robin	US	richly organic	part shade to shade
Veronica	speedwell	US	well-drained, organic	sun to part shade

GROUNDCOVERS

GENUS	COMMON NAME	ORIGINS	GARDEN SOIL TYPE	EXPOSURE
Aegopodium	bishop's weed	Eurasia	adaptable	part sun to part shade
Ajuga	carpet bugle	UK	adaptable	part sun to part shade
Arctostaphylos	bearberry	US west	adaptable	sun to part shade
Epimedium	fairy wings	Asia, Europe south	well-drained	sun to part shade
Heuchera	coral bells	North America	adaptable	part sun to part shade
Lamium	yellow archangel	Europe, Asia	adaptable	part sun to part shade
Leptinella	leptinella	New Zealand	adaptable	part sun to part shade
Liriope	lily turf	Asia	adaptable	sun to shade
Lysimachia	moneywort	Eurasia	adaptable	sun to shade
Pachysandra	pachysandra	Asia	adaptable	part sun to shade
Pennisetum	little bunny	Africa, Asia	well-drained	sun
Pulmonaria	lungwort	Europe	well-drained	sun to part shade
Rubus	creeping raspberry	US west	well-drained, organic	part sun to part shade
Sedum	sedum	North America, Europe	well-drained	sun to part sun
Stachys	lamb's ear	Europe	well-drained	part sun to part shade
Woodsia	hardy fern	US	richly organic	part shade to shade

WATER	FERTILIZER	PRUNING
grow on dry side	flowering perennial formula in spring	remove spent flowers
regularly	flowering perennial formula in spring	remove spent flowers, cut back when dormant
grow on dry side	flowering perennial formula in spring	remove spent flowers, cut back when dormant
grow on dry side	flowering perennial formula in spring	remove spent flowers, cut back when dormant
grow on dry side	flowering perennial formula in spring	remove spent flowers, cut back when dormant
grow on dry side	flowering perennial formula in spring	remove spent flowers
regularly	perennial formula in spring and summer	remove spent flowers
regularly	flowering perennial formula in spring	remove spent flowers, cut back when dormant
regularly	flowering perennial formula in spring, summer	remove spent flower stalks
regularly	flowering perennial formula in summer	remove spent flower stalks
regularly	flowering perennial formula in summer	remove spent flower stalks
regularly	flowering perennial formula in spring	remove spent flowers, cut back when dormant
grow on dry side	perennial formula in spring and summer	remove spent flowers, cut back when dormant
grow on dry side	perennial formula in spring and summer	remove spent flowers
regularly	perennial formula in spring and summer	remove spent flowers
regularly in summer	flowering perennial formula in spring	remove spent flowers, cut back when dormant
regularly	flowering perennial formula in spring	remove spent flowers
regularly	flowering perennial formula in spring, summer	
regularly	perennial formula in spring and summer	cut back when dormant
grow on dry side	perennial formula in spring and summer	trim back in spring
grow on dry side	flowering perennial formula in spring, summer	remove spent flower stalks
regularly	flowering perennial formula in spring, summer	remove spent flower stalks
regularly	flowering perennial formula in spring	remove spent flower stalks or let reseed
regularly	flowering perennial formula in spring	remove spent flowers
regularly in summer	flowering perennial formula in spring	remove spent flowers
grow on dry side	perennial formula in spring and summer	shear off spent flowers
grow on dry side	perennial formula in spring and summer	shear off spent flowers
grow on dry side	perennial formula in spring and summer	cut back to control spread
regularly	flowering perennial formula in spring	shear off spent flowers
regularly in summer	perennial formula in spring and summer	remove spent flowers and leaves
regularly in summer	flowering perennial formula in spring	remove spent flowers
regularly in summer	perennial formula in spring and summer	cut back to control spread
grow on dry side	perennial formula in spring and summer	cut back in late winter
grow on dry side	perennial formula in spring and summer	cut back to control spread
regularly	perennial formula in spring and summer	cut back to control spread
grow on dry side	perennial formula in spring and summer	cut back after flowering
grow on dry side	perennial formula in spring and summer	cut back to control spread
regularly	perennial formula in spring and summer	cut back to control spread
grow on dry side	perennial formula in spring and summer	cut back after flowering
regularly in summer	perennial formula in spring and summer	cut back after flowering
regularly	perennial formula in spring and summer	cut back spent fronds

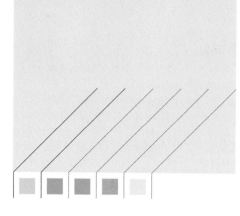

More colorful plants

IN ADDITION TO THE PLANTS PROFILED in this book, there are many others that can deliver buckets of color. Here are more to consider as you bring top-down, year-round color to your garden.

ANNUAL FLOWERS

Every locality has must-have annual flowers that every gardener enjoys each year; use this list to expand your color collection. Because the range of annuals is so great, and can change so rapidly, use this list as a starting point but check out all the options for your area.

Bacopa • *Sutera cordata*

Cape Daisy • *Osterspermum* hybrids

Cleome • *Cleome hassleriana* and hybrids

Creeping Zinnia • *Sanvitalia* species

Fan Flower • *Scaevola aemula* and hybrids

Lobelia • *Lobelia erinus* and hybrids

Marguerite Daisy • *Argyranthemum frutescens*

Nemesia • *Nemesia fruticans* and hybrids

Strawflower • *Bracteantha* species

Summer Snapdragon • *Angelonia angustifolia* hybrids

Superbells • *Calibrachoa* hybrids

Twinspur • *Diascia* hybrids

OUTSTANDING BARKS

Tree bark colors add winter interest, but also unify the landscape through the seasons.

Birch-bark Cherry • *Prunus serrula*

Bois d'Arc • *Maclura pomifera*

Himalayan White Birch • *Betula utilis jacquemontii*

Honey Locust • *Gleditsia triacanthos*

Lacebark Pine • *Pinus bungeana*

Manchurian Stripebark Maple • *Acer tegmentosum* 'Joe Witt'

Seven-Sons Plant • *Heptacodium miconioides*

Weeping Blue Cedar • *Chamaecyparis nootkatensis* 'Glauca Pendula'

WILD VARIEGATION

When you're looking for just the right eye-catcher to add contrast to the garden scene, check this list. Many of their common names begin with their designation, as in "variegated butterfly bush."

TREES

Alleycat Redbud • *Cercis canadensis* 'Alley Cat'

Giant Dogwood • *Cornus controversa* 'Variegata'

Hinoki Cypress • *Chamaecyparis obtusa* 'Aurea'

Silver Sweetgum • *Liquidamber* 'Silver King'

Snakebark • *Acer conspicuum* 'Esk Flamingo'

SHRUBS

Beautyberry • *Callicarpa japonica* 'Variegata'

Bollywood Azalea • *Rhododendron* 'Bollywood'

Butterfly Bush • *Buddleia* 'Summer Skies'

Daphne • *Daphne* 'Silver Edge'

Pieris • *Pieris* 'Passion Frost'

PERENNIALS

Capri Joe-Pye • *Eupatorium* 'Capri'

Columbine • *Aquilegia* 'Leprechaun'

Double Stuff • *Polygonatum* 'Variegatum'

Frosted Joe-Pye • *Eupatorium* 'Frosted Elegance'

Lungwort • *Pulmonaria* 'Silver Bouquet'

Purple Dragon • *Lamium maculatum* 'Purple Dragon

GROUNDCOVERS

Callaway Ginger • *Asarum shuttleworthii* 'Callaway'

Edgehog • *Dianthus* 'Edgehog'

Emerald Mist • *Brunnera* 'Emerald Mist'

Fragrant Star • *Erysimum* 'Fragrant Star'

Gold Fairy Bells • *Prosartes hookeri*
   (formerly *Disporum* genus)

Great Masterwort • *Astrantia* 'Vanilla Gorilla'

SHRUBS FOR CONTAINERS

Your signature color can shine in big containers, and the addition of small shrubs enhances their impact. Not surprisingly, their common names all begin with the word "dwarf."

Bluebeard • *Caryopteris incana* 'Sunshine Blue'

Blueblossom • *Ceanothus thyrsiflorus repens*

Blue Sargent Juniper • *Juniperus chinensis sargentii* 'Glauca'

Shrubby Veronica • *Hebes odora*

Weigela • *Weigela* 'My Monet'

Reading List

FOR MORE INFORMATION about topics and plants addressed in this book, consult these references.

Armitage, Allan M. *Armitage's Garden Annuals: A Color Encyclopedia.* Portland, OR: Timber Press, 2004.

Courtright, Gordon. *Trees and Shrubs for Temperate Climates.* Portland: Timber Press, 1979.

Dirr, Michael A. *Dirr's Hardy Trees and Shrubs.* Portland: Timber Press, 1997.

———. *Dirr's Trees and Shrubs for Warm Climates: An Illustrated Encyclopedia.* Portland: Timber Press, 2002.

———. *Viburnums: Flowering Shrubs for Every Season.* Portland: Timber Press, 2007.

Ellis, Barbara. *Covering Ground: Unexpected Ideas for Landscaping.* North Adams, MA: Storey Publishing, 2007.

Hériteau, Thomas, Charles, and Jacqueline. *Water Gardens.* Boston: Houghton Mifflin Harcourt, 1996.

Martin, Laura C. *Gardens of the Heartland.* New York: Abbeville Press, 1996.

Odenwald, Neil and James R. Turner. *Identification, Selection, and Use of Southern Plants,* 4th rev. ed. Baton Rouge: Claitor's Law Books and Publishing, 2010.

Ogden, Scott and Lauren S. *Plant Driven Design.* Portland: Timber Press, 2008.

Rice, Graham, editor-in-chief. *AHS Encyclopedia of Garden Perennials.* New York: DK Publishing, 2006.

von Trapp, Sara Jane. *Landscaping from the Ground Up.* Newtown, CT: Taunton Books, 1997.

Photo Credits

Andre Viette: 157 (Clematis)

Annie's Annuals & Perennials: 171 (Brass Buttons)

Arthur Chapman: 169 (Bunchberry)

Bruce Marlin: 139 (Fragrant Sumac)

Charles Mann: 153 (Beardtongue)

Drew Avery: 164 (Great Globe Thistle)

Gary Irish: 114 (Desert Willow)

George Weigel: 43, 52, 57, 58, 61, 62, 74, 79 (top), 83, 84, 90, 91, 92, 93, 96, 107 (Harlequin Glorybower), 111 (Pendant Silver Linden), 121 (American Hophornbeam), 122 (Japanese Zelkova), 126 (right), 131 (Ninebark), 132 (Red Osier Dogwood), 137 (Dyer's Greenwood), 146 (Chinese Photinia), 147 (Pearlbush), 147 (Slender Deutzia), 166, 170 (Stonecrop)

Jerry Pavia: 98, 101 (left), 104 (Kwanzan Cherry), 105 (Chaste Tree), 110 (Golden Chain Tree), 112 (Quaking Aspen), 112 (Sassafras), 123 (River Birch), 124, 125 (left), 125 (right), 126 (left), 128 (left), 128 (right), 130 (Japanese Barberry), 132 (Shrub Rose), 135 (Purple Beautyberry), 140 (Witch Hazel), 141 (Evergreen Euonymus), 149 (right), 149 (left), 150 (left), 150 (right), 154 (Columbine), 155 (Peony), 158 (Joe-Pye Weed), 160 (Blanket Flower), 161 (Lady Fern), 168 (left), 168 (right), 172 (Creeping Raspberry), 174 (Yellow Archangel)

© judywhite/GardenPhotos.com: 5, 6, 36, 39, 50, 59, 64, 66, 71, 72, 80 (bottom), 87, 94, 148

© iStockPhoto: 9 (BasieB); 11 (StukChocolate); 13 (David A. Birkbeck); 14 (chinaface); 16 (Jeanne McRight); 19 (Ron and Patty Thomas Photography); 21 (Ogphoto); 76 (Kings Photo); 80, top (Verena Matthew); 81, left (JenniferPhotographyImaging); 81, right (rodho); 82 (RoseABC); 88 (Adventure Photo); 89 (Ruth Black)

Lee Anne White: 56, 73

Liz Ball: 101 (right), 103 (Blackgum), 113 (Bald Cypress), 115 (Eastern Red Cedar), 129 (Burkwood Daphne), 144 (Summersweet), 145 (Annabelle Hydrangea), 154 (Cardinal Flower), 173 (Moneywort), 174 (Lily Turf)

Pam Harper: 137 (Sweetshrub)

Peter Etchells/Dreamstime.com: 127 (left)

Ralph Snodsmith: 138 (Forsythia)

Richard Shiell, courtesy Monrovia: 129 (Flowering Quince)

Shutterstock: 25, bottom right (stavklem); 26 (maturos1812); 27 (Jamie Hooper); 28, top (Igor Sokolov); 28, bottom (MarKord); 29 (I love photo); 30 (Arkadia); 31 (Denise Lett); 32 (Marty Pitcairn); 32, bottom left (Nop Inu); 32, top (Robert Crum); 34 (leoks); 35, bottom left (Francesco De Marco); 35, top left (Guzel Studio); 35, right (Poly Liss); 45 (Greg Kieca); 49 (white78); 65 (smikeymikey1); 78 (Razvan Bucur); 79, bottom (Nir Levy); 85, left (karamysh); 95 (Antonina Potapenko); 99, right (Kathy Clark); 100, left (Stephen Farhall); 102, left (Hintau Aliaksei); 103, Korean Stewartia (Jorge Salcedo); 106, Eastern Redbud (Betty Shelton) and Empress Tree (Flaviano Fabrizi); 108, Rose of Sharon (Ralf Neumann); 109, Sweetgum (Stephanie Frey); 110, Gingko (Inomoto); 113, Tulip Poplar (belkxu); 119, Flowering Crabapple (Kenneth Keifer); 119, Flowering Dogwood (Steven Russell Smith Photos); 120, Sycamore (Borodaev); 121, Crape Myrtle (TRE Wheeler BA Hons); 122, Downy Serviceberry (Joan Budai); 134, French Hybrid Ceanothus (Michaelpuche); 146, Glossy Abelia (alybaba); 151, right (alybaba); 155, Garden Phlox (weter 777); 160, Daylily (freya-photographer); 163, Wake Robin (Flora Ehrlich); 165, Knotweed (Martin Fowler); 169, Bearberry (LFRabanedo); 170, Cinquefoil (Alesikka)

The Sir Harold Hillier Gardens: 33

Thomas Eltzroth: 85 (right), 86, 100 (right), 102 (right), 104 (Smoketree), 105 (Strawbery Tree), 108 (Purple-Leaf Plum), 109 (Chinese Pistache), 111 (Golden Raintree), 114 (Dawn Redwood), 115 (Japanese Privet), 116 (Lacebark Elm), 116 (Pines), 117 (Weeping Willow), 118 (Catalpa), 120 (Star Magnolia), 123 (Paperbark Maple), 133 (Blue Mist Shrub), 133 (Spreading Cotoneaster), 135 (Oregon Grapeholly), 139 (Japanese Kerria), 141 (Chinese Juniper), 142 (Fatsia), 142 (Heavenly Bamboo), 143 (Japanese Pieris), 143 (Sasanqua), 144 (Adam's Needle Yucca), 151 (left), 152 (left), 152 (right), 153 (Astilbe), 156 (Pinks), 157 (Gayfeather), 158 (Speedwell), 159 (Black-Eyed Susan), 162 (Rosemary), 162 (Shield Fern), 163 (Candytuft), 164 (Eulalia Grass), 165 (Shasta Daisy), 167 (left), 167 (right), 171 (Carpet Bugle), 172 (Lungwort), 173 (Fairy Wings), 175 (Bishop's Weed), 175 (Pachysandra), 176 (Lamb's Ear), 176 (Dwarf Fountain Grass)

Troy Marden: 117 (Blackhaw), 136 (Redleaf Loropetalum), 156 (Purple Coneflower), 159 (Stokes' Aster), 161 (Sundrops)

Wikimedia/Creative Commons: 99, left (H. Zell); 107, Pawpaw (Krzysztof Ziarnek); 118, Castor-Aralia (Dalgial); 127, right (Nova); 130, Mountain Laurel (Bottville); 131, Piedmont Azalea (Daderot); 134, Meyer Lilac (Daderot); 136, Purple Giant Filbert (Marcus Cyron); 138, Fothergilla (Jean-Pol Grandmont); 140, Tangerine Cinquefoil (Opioła Jerzy); 145, Chinese Fringe Flower (KENPEI)

Index

Meet Nellie Neal

NELLIE NEAL IS A GARDEN WRITER AND RADIO HOST whose work has appeared in a variety of media platforms for more than two decades. She chose her first plant at age 8, a begonia with a red flower the same color as nail polish she wasn't allowed to wear. She went on to earn a BS degree from LSU where she studied her mutual passions, English and horticulture. Nellie's personal style is reflected in her garden, and both have been called geeky and eccentric, but always colorful!

After years in California and southern Louisiana, Nellie found a home in central Mississippi and began her radio programs and website, gardenmama.com. Today, gardeners ask "GardenMama" questions and she answers on radio, online, and in print. She is a serious advocate and practitioner of lifelong, year-round gardening who says the kindest compliment is to hear that her advice worked. When she takes a break from gardening with her husband, Dave Ingram, she visits friends, family, and gardens, haunts thrift stores, and works crossword puzzles.

Nellie is the author of *Deep South Month-by-Month Gardening* (Cool Springs Press, 2014); *Gardener's Guide to Tropical Plants* (Cool Springs Press, 2012); *Questions and Answers for Deep South Gardeners, 1st and 2nd eds.* (B. B. Mackey Books, 2002 and 2010); *Organic Gardening Down South* (B. B. Mackey Books, 2008); *Getting Started in Southern Gardening* (Cool Springs Press, 2005); *GardenMama, Tell Me Why* (G2C Books, 2004); and *The Garden Primer* (Loose Dirt Publishing, 1999). She has also served as contributing editor for *Ortho's All About Houseplants* and *Ortho's All About Greenhouses* and as a contributing writer for *Annuals for Dummies* and *Rodale's Low Maintenance Gardening*.

She is a member of the Garden Writers Association, the Mississippi Nursery and Landscape Association, and the Mississippi Sustainable Agriculture Network.